Knowledge Quiz

Chemistry

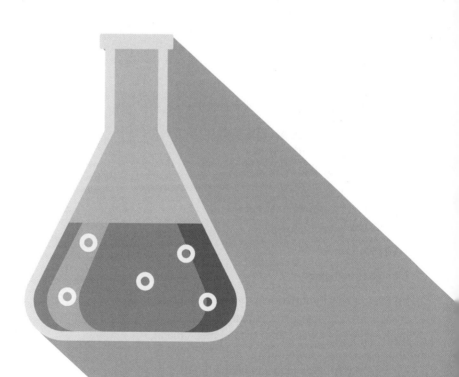

Adam Boxer

First published 2019

by John Catt Educational Ltd,
15 Riduna Park, Station Road,
Melton, Woodbridge IP12 1QT

Tel: +44 (0) 1394 389850
Email: enquiries@johncatt.com
Website: www.johncatt.com

ISBN: 9781912906130

Set and designed by John Catt Educational Ltd

How to use this book

1	Start with Section 1. Use the answer key to memorise the facts and formulae in that section.
2	If you see anything unfamiliar make sure you look it up or ask your teacher about it.
3	When you're ready complete the first quiz from memory.
4	Mark it using the answer key.
5	Record your score in the section tracker.
6	Leave it a few days, then try the same quiz again.
7	Keep completing the same quiz every few days until you get full marks every time.
8	Move onto the next section and repeat steps 1 – 8.
9	Revisit previously mastered sections after a few weeks or months to check you still know the content.

Which quizzes should I complete?

✓ Students studying Double Award Science should complete Sections 1 – 25.

✓ Students studying Triple Award Science should complete Sections 1 – 34.

✓ Questions marked (HT) contain Higher tier content. This knowledge is not required for the Foundation tier.

Important!

This book will help you memorise most of the facts and formulae that you need to know for your chemistry GCSE. There are many other things you need to do to prepare for your exams – including lots and lots of practice. Memorising facts and formulae gives you the fundamental knowledge you need, and being able to apply that knowledge is the next challenge.

Contents

Section	Started?	Achieved 100%?	Revisited?
1. Atomic Structure and Periodic Table 1			
2. Atomic Structure and Periodic Table 2			
3. Atomic Structure and Periodic Table 3			
4. Atomic Structure and Periodic Table 4			
5. Bonding and Structure 1			
6. Bonding and Structure 2			
7. Bonding and Structure 3			
8. Quantitative Chemistry			
9. Chemical Changes 1			
10. Chemical Changes 2			
11. Chemical Changes 3			
12. Chemical Changes 4			
13. Energy Changes			
14. Rate of Reaction 1			
15. Rate of Reaction 2			
16. Reversible Reactions			
17. Organic Chemistry 1			
18. Organic Chemistry 2			
19. Chemical Analysis 1			
20. Chemical Analysis 2			
21. Chemistry of the Atmosphere 1			
22. Chemistry of the Atmosphere 2			
23. Chemistry of the Atmosphere 3			
24. The Earth's Resources 1			
25. The Earth's Resources 2			
Triple Content			
26. Transition Metals & Nanoparticles			
27. Further Quantitative			
28. Chemical and Fuel Cells			
29. Further Organic - Alkenes			
30. Further Organic - Alkenes and Carboxylic Acids 1			
31. Further Organic - Alkenes and Carboxylic Acids 2			
32. Identification of Ions 1			
33. Identification of Ions 2 & Using Materials 1			
34. Using Materials 2			

Section 1: Atomic Structure and Periodic Table 1

ANSWER KEY

1.1	What is an atom?	The smallest part of an element that can exist
1.2	What is an element?	A substance made of only one type of atom
1.3	What is a compound?	A substance made of two or more different atoms chemically bonded together
1.4	How are compounds formed?	From chemical reactions
1.5	What is involved in a chemical reaction?	The formation of one or more new substances and an energy change
1.6	What is a molecule?	A substance made of more than one atom chemically bonded together
1.7	What is a mixture?	A substance made of more than one thing not chemically bonded together
1.8	How can mixtures be separated?	Physical processes (filtration, crystallisation, simple distillation, fractional distillation and chromatography)
1.9	Name the three subatomic particles	Protons, neutrons, electrons
1.10	State the relative masses and charges of the subatomic particles	Mass: Protons: 1, neutrons: 1, electrons: 0. Charge: Protons: +1, neutrons: 0, electrons: -1
1.11	What is the plum pudding model of the atom?	A ball of positive charge with negative electrons studded into it
1.12	What did the gold foil experiment (alpha particle scattering) prove?	That atoms have dense nucleuses with a positive charge

TRACKER

Quiz	Date	Score
1		
2		
3		
4		
5		
6		

Got it? ☐

1.1	What is an atom?	
1.2	What is an element?	
1.3	What is a compound?	
1.4	How are compounds formed?	
1.5	What is involved in a chemical reaction?	
1.6	What is a molecule?	
1.7	What is a mixture?	
1.8	How can mixtures be separated?	
1.9	Name the three subatomic particles	
1.10	State the relative masses and charges of the subatomic particles	
1.11	What is the plum pudding model of the atom?	
1.12	What did the gold foil experiment (alpha particle scattering) prove?	

1.1	What is an atom?	
1.2	What is an element?	
1.3	What is a compound?	
1.4	How are compounds formed?	
1.5	What is involved in a chemical reaction?	
1.6	What is a molecule?	
1.7	What is a mixture?	
1.8	How can mixtures be separated?	
1.9	Name the three subatomic particles	
1.10	State the relative masses and charges of the subatomic particles	
1.11	What is the plum pudding model of the atom?	
1.12	What did the gold foil experiment (alpha particle scattering) prove?	

1.1	What is an atom?	
1.2	What is an element?	
1.3	What is a compound?	
1.4	How are compounds formed?	
1.5	What is involved in a chemical reaction?	
1.6	What is a molecule?	
1.7	What is a mixture?	
1.8	How can mixtures be separated?	
1.9	Name the three subatomic particles	
1.10	State the relative masses and charges of the subatomic particles	
1.11	What is the plum pudding model of the atom?	
1.12	What did the gold foil experiment (alpha particle scattering) prove?	

1.1	What is an atom?	
1.2	What is an element?	
1.3	What is a compound?	
1.4	How are compounds formed?	
1.5	What is involved in a chemical reaction?	
1.6	What is a molecule?	
1.7	What is a mixture?	
1.8	How can mixtures be separated?	
1.9	Name the three subatomic particles	
1.10	State the relative masses and charges of the subatomic particles	
1.11	What is the plum pudding model of the atom?	
1.12	What did the gold foil experiment (alpha particle scattering) prove?	

Section 1: Atomic Structure and Periodic Table 1

1.1	What is an atom?	
1.2	What is an element?	
1.3	What is a compound?	
1.4	How are compounds formed?	
1.5	What is involved in a chemical reaction?	
1.6	What is a molecule?	
1.7	What is a mixture?	
1.8	How can mixtures be separated?	
1.9	Name the three subatomic particles	
1.10	State the relative masses and charges of the subatomic particles	
1.11	What is the plum pudding model of the atom?	
1.12	What did the gold foil experiment (alpha particle scattering) prove?	

1.1	What is an atom?	
1.2	What is an element?	
1.3	What is a compound?	
1.4	How are compounds formed?	
1.5	What is involved in a chemical reaction?	
1.6	What is a molecule?	
1.7	What is a mixture?	
1.8	How can mixtures be separated?	
1.9	Name the three subatomic particles	
1.10	State the relative masses and charges of the subatomic particles	
1.11	What is the plum pudding model of the atom?	
1.12	What did the gold foil experiment (alpha particle scattering) prove?	

ANSWER KEY

2.1	What did Chadwick discover?	The neutron
2.2	What did Bohr's experiments show?	That electrons are in specific shells
2.3	What is the atomic number of an atom?	The number of protons in an atom
2.4	What is the mass number of an atom?	The number of protons + the number of neutrons in an atom
2.5	In the electron shell model, how are the subatomic particles arranged in an atom?	Protons and neutrons in the nucleus, electrons orbiting in shells
2.6	Why is the number of electrons in an atom equal to the number of protons?	As their charges cancel out
2.7	How many electrons can go in the first shell?	2
2.8	How many electrons can go in the second and third shells?	8
2.9	What are groups in the periodic table?	The columns, numbered 1, 2, 3, 4, 5, 6, 7, 0
2.10	What can the group tell you about the electrons in an atom?	How many electrons in the outer shell. E.g. carbon is in group 4 so has 4 electrons in the outer shell
2.11	What are periods in the periodic table?	The rows in the periodic table
2.12	What can the period tell you about the electrons in an atom?	How many shells an atom has. E.g. carbon is in the second period so has two shells

TRACKER

Quiz	Date	Score
1		
2		
3		
4		
5		
6		

Got it? ☐

2.1	What did Chadwick discover?	
2.2	What did Bohr's experiments show?	
2.3	What is the atomic number of an atom?	
2.4	What is the mass number of an atom?	
2.5	In the electron shell model, how are the subatomic particles arranged in an atom?	
2.6	Why is the number of electrons in an atom equal to the number of protons?	
2.7	How many electrons can go in the first shell?	
2.8	How many electrons can go in the second and third shells?	
2.9	What are groups in the periodic table?	
2.10	What can the group tell you about the electrons in an atom?	
2.11	What are periods in the periodic table?	
2.12	What can the period tell you about the electrons in an atom?	

2.1	What did Chadwick discover?	
2.2	What did Bohr's experiments show?	
2.3	What is the atomic number of an atom?	
2.4	What is the mass number of an atom?	
2.5	In the electron shell model, how are the subatomic particles arranged in an atom?	
2.6	Why is the number of electrons in an atom equal to the number of protons?	
2.7	How many electrons can go in the first shell?	
2.8	How many electrons can go in the second and third shells?	
2.9	What are groups in the periodic table?	
2.10	What can the group tell you about the electrons in an atom?	
2.11	What are periods in the periodic table?	
2.12	What can the period tell you about the electrons in an atom?	

Section 2: Atomic Structure and Periodic Table 2

2.1	What did Chadwick discover?	
2.2	What did Bohr's experiments show?	
2.3	What is the atomic number of an atom?	
2.4	What is the mass number of an atom?	
2.5	In the electron shell model, how are the subatomic particles arranged in an atom?	
2.6	Why is the number of electrons in an atom equal to the number of protons?	
2.7	How many electrons can go in the first shell?	
2.8	How many electrons can go in the second and third shells?	
2.9	What are groups in the periodic table?	
2.10	What can the group tell you about the electrons in an atom?	
2.11	What are periods in the periodic table?	
2.12	What can the period tell you about the electrons in an atom?	

2.1	What did Chadwick discover?	
2.2	What did Bohr's experiments show?	
2.3	What is the atomic number of an atom?	
2.4	What is the mass number of an atom?	
2.5	In the electron shell model, how are the subatomic particles arranged in an atom?	
2.6	Why is the number of electrons in an atom equal to the number of protons?	
2.7	How many electrons can go in the first shell?	
2.8	How many electrons can go in the second and third shells?	
2.9	What are groups in the periodic table?	
2.10	What can the group tell you about the electrons in an atom?	
2.11	What are periods in the periodic table?	
2.12	What can the period tell you about the electrons in an atom?	

2.1	What did Chadwick discover?	
2.2	What did Bohr's experiments show?	
2.3	What is the atomic number of an atom?	
2.4	What is the mass number of an atom?	
2.5	In the electron shell model, how are the subatomic particles arranged in an atom?	
2.6	Why is the number of electrons in an atom equal to the number of protons?	
2.7	How many electrons can go in the first shell?	
2.8	How many electrons can go in the second and third shells?	
2.9	What are groups in the periodic table?	
2.10	What can the group tell you about the electrons in an atom?	
2.11	What are periods in the periodic table?	
2.12	What can the period tell you about the electrons in an atom?	

2.1	What did Chadwick discover?	
2.2	What did Bohr's experiments show?	
2.3	What is the atomic number of an atom?	
2.4	What is the mass number of an atom?	
2.5	In the electron shell model, how are the subatomic particles arranged in an atom?	
2.6	Why is the number of electrons in an atom equal to the number of protons?	
2.7	How many electrons can go in the first shell?	
2.8	How many electrons can go in the second and third shells?	
2.9	What are groups in the periodic table?	
2.10	What can the group tell you about the electrons in an atom?	
2.11	What are periods in the periodic table?	
2.12	What can the period tell you about the electrons in an atom?	

Section 3: Atomic Structure and Periodic Table 3

ANSWER KEY

3.1	Why do atoms have no overall charge?	The number of electrons and protons are equal
3.2	Approximately how large are atoms?	Radius is about 0.1nm
3.3	How large is the nucleus compared to the whole atom?	About 1/10000 the size
3.4	What are isotopes?	Atoms of the same element with a different number of neutrons
3.5	What is abundance?	The % of atoms in a sample with a particular mass
3.6	What is the relative atomic mass of an element?	An average value for the mass that takes account of the abundance of the isotopes of the element
3.7	In the modern periodic table, how are the atoms arranged?	By their atomic number and in groups according to chemical properties
3.8	Why do elements in the same group have similar chemical properties?	Because they have the same number of electrons in their outer shell
3.9	Before the discovery of protons, neutrons and electrons, how did scientists organise the elements?	By their atomic weight
3.10	Why did Mendeleev leave gaps in his periodic table?	For elements that had not yet been discovered
3.11	Which discovery meant that organising elements by their atomic weight not always correct?	Isotopes
3.12	Where are metals on the periodic table found?	To the left and bottom of the periodic table

TRACKER

Quiz	Date	Score
1		
2		
3		
4		
5		
6		

Got it? ☐

3.1	Why do atoms have no overall charge?	
3.2	Approximately how large are atoms?	
3.3	How large is the nucleus compared to the whole atom?	
3.4	What are isotopes?	
3.5	What is abundance?	
3.6	What is the relative atomic mass of an element?	
3.7	In the modern periodic table, how are the atoms arranged?	
3.8	Why do elements in the same group have similar chemical properties?	
3.9	Before the discovery of protons, neutrons and electrons, how did scientists organise the elements?	
3.10	Why did Mendeleev leave gaps in his periodic table?	
3.11	Which discovery meant that organising elements by their atomic weight not always correct?	
3.12	Where are metals on the periodic table found?	

3.1	Why do atoms have no overall charge?	
3.2	Approximately how large are atoms?	
3.3	How large is the nucleus compared to the whole atom?	
3.4	What are isotopes?	
3.5	What is abundance?	
3.6	What is the relative atomic mass of an element?	
3.7	In the modern periodic table, how are the atoms arranged?	
3.8	Why do elements in the same group have similar chemical properties?	
3.9	Before the discovery of protons, neutrons and electrons, how did scientists organise the elements?	
3.10	Why did Mendeleev leave gaps in his periodic table?	
3.11	Which discovery meant that organising elements by their atomic weight not always correct?	
3.12	Where are metals on the periodic table found?	

3.1	Why do atoms have no overall charge?	
3.2	Approximately how large are atoms?	
3.3	How large is the nucleus compared to the whole atom?	
3.4	What are isotopes?	
3.5	What is abundance?	
3.6	What is the relative atomic mass of an element?	
3.7	In the modern periodic table, how are the atoms arranged?	
3.8	Why do elements in the same group have similar chemical properties?	
3.9	Before the discovery of protons, neutrons and electrons, how did scientists organise the elements?	
3.10	Why did Mendeleev leave gaps in his periodic table?	
3.11	Which discovery meant that organising elements by their atomic weight not always correct?	
3.12	Where are metals on the periodic table found?	

3.1	Why do atoms have no overall charge?	
3.2	Approximately how large are atoms?	
3.3	How large is the nucleus compared to the whole atom?	
3.4	What are isotopes?	
3.5	What is abundance?	
3.6	What is the relative atomic mass of an element?	
3.7	In the modern periodic table, how are the atoms arranged?	
3.8	Why do elements in the same group have similar chemical properties?	
3.9	Before the discovery of protons, neutrons and electrons, how did scientists organise the elements?	
3.10	Why did Mendeleev leave gaps in his periodic table?	
3.11	Which discovery meant that organising elements by their atomic weight not always correct?	
3.12	Where are metals on the periodic table found?	

3.1	Why do atoms have no overall charge?	
3.2	Approximately how large are atoms?	
3.3	How large is the nucleus compared to the whole atom?	
3.4	What are isotopes?	
3.5	What is abundance?	
3.6	What is the relative atomic mass of an element?	
3.7	In the modern periodic table, how are the atoms arranged?	
3.8	Why do elements in the same group have similar chemical properties?	
3.9	Before the discovery of protons, neutrons and electrons, how did scientists organise the elements?	
3.10	Why did Mendeleev leave gaps in his periodic table?	
3.11	Which discovery meant that organising elements by their atomic weight not always correct?	
3.12	Where are metals on the periodic table found?	

3.1	Why do atoms have no overall charge?	
3.2	Approximately how large are atoms?	
3.3	How large is the nucleus compared to the whole atom?	
3.4	What are isotopes?	
3.5	What is abundance?	
3.6	What is the relative atomic mass of an element?	
3.7	In the modern periodic table, how are the atoms arranged?	
3.8	Why do elements in the same group have similar chemical properties?	
3.9	Before the discovery of protons, neutrons and electrons, how did scientists organise the elements?	
3.10	Why did Mendeleev leave gaps in his periodic table?	
3.11	Which discovery meant that organising elements by their atomic weight not always correct?	
3.12	Where are metals on the periodic table found?	

Section 4: Atomic Structure and Periodic Table 4

ANSWER KEY

4.1	What is an ion?	An atom which has lost or gained electrons
4.2	What kinds of ions do metals and non-metals form?	Metals form positive, non-metals form negative
4.3	What name is given to elements in group 0?	Noble gases
4.4	Why are the group 0 elements unreactive?	They have full outer shells so do not need to lose or gain electrons
4.5	How does the boiling point of group 0 elements change down the group?	Increases down the group
4.6	Explain why the group 1 elements are called alkali metals	They are metals that form alkalis when they react with water
4.7	What are the products of the alkali metals in a reaction with: oxygen, water, halogen?	Oxygen: metal oxide, Water: metal hydroxide + hydrogen, Halogen: metal halide
4.8	Explain why the group 1 elements get more reactive down the group	More electrons, more shielding, weaker electrostatic attraction from the nucleus to the outer shell, easier to lose an electron
4.9	What name is given to elements in group 7?	Halogens
4.10	How does the boiling point of group 7 elements change down the group?	Increases down the group
4.11	Explain why the group 7 elements get less reactive down the group	More electrons, more shielding, weaker electrostatic attraction from the nucleus to the outer shell, harder to gain an electron
4.12	What is a displacement reaction?	Where a more reactive element displaces a less reactive one from a compound

TRACKER

Quiz	Date	Score
1		
2		
3		
4		
5		
6		

Got it? ☐

4.1	What is an ion?	
4.2	What kinds of ions do metals and non-metals form?	
4.3	What name is given to elements in group 0?	
4.4	Why are the group 0 elements unreactive?	
4.5	How does the boiling point of group 0 elements change down the group?	
4.6	Explain why the group 1 elements are called alkali metals	
4.7	What are the products of the alkali metals in a reaction with: oxygen, water, halogen?	
4.8	Explain why the group 1 elements get more reactive down the group	
4.9	What name is given to elements in group 7?	
4.10	How does the boiling point of group 7 elements change down the group?	
4.11	Explain why the group 7 elements get less reactive down the group	
4.12	What is a displacement reaction?	

4.1	What is an ion?	
4.2	What kinds of ions do metals and non-metals form?	
4.3	What name is given to elements in group 0?	
4.4	Why are the group 0 elements unreactive?	
4.5	How does the boiling point of group 0 elements change down the group?	
4.6	Explain why the group 1 elements are called alkali metals	
4.7	What are the products of the alkali metals in a reaction with: oxygen, water, halogen?	
4.8	Explain why the group 1 elements get more reactive down the group	
4.9	What name is given to elements in group 7?	
4.10	How does the boiling point of group 7 elements change down the group?	
4.11	Explain why the group 7 elements get less reactive down the group	
4.12	What is a displacement reaction?	

4.1	What is an ion?	
4.2	What kinds of ions do metals and non-metals form?	
4.3	What name is given to elements in group 0?	
4.4	Why are the group 0 elements unreactive?	
4.5	How does the boiling point of group 0 elements change down the group?	
4.6	Explain why the group 1 elements are called alkali metals	
4.7	What are the products of the alkali metals in a reaction with: oxygen, water, halogen?	
4.8	Explain why the group 1 elements get more reactive down the group	
4.9	What name is given to elements in group 7?	
4.10	How does the boiling point of group 7 elements change down the group?	
4.11	Explain why the group 7 elements get less reactive down the group	
4.12	What is a displacement reaction?	

4.1	What is an ion?	
4.2	What kinds of ions do metals and non-metals form?	
4.3	What name is given to elements in group 0?	
4.4	Why are the group 0 elements unreactive?	
4.5	How does the boiling point of group 0 elements change down the group?	
4.6	Explain why the group 1 elements are called alkali metals	
4.7	What are the products of the alkali metals in a reaction with: oxygen, water, halogen?	
4.8	Explain why the group 1 elements get more reactive down the group	
4.9	What name is given to elements in group 7?	
4.10	How does the boiling point of group 7 elements change down the group?	
4.11	Explain why the group 7 elements get less reactive down the group	
4.12	What is a displacement reaction?	

4.1	What is an ion?	
4.2	What kinds of ions do metals and non-metals form?	
4.3	What name is given to elements in group 0?	
4.4	Why are the group 0 elements unreactive?	
4.5	How does the boiling point of group 0 elements change down the group?	
4.6	Explain why the group 1 elements are called alkali metals	
4.7	What are the products of the alkali metals in a reaction with: oxygen, water, halogen?	
4.8	Explain why the group 1 elements get more reactive down the group	
4.9	What name is given to elements in group 7?	
4.10	How does the boiling point of group 7 elements change down the group?	
4.11	Explain why the group 7 elements get less reactive down the group	
4.12	What is a displacement reaction?	

4.1	What is an ion?	
4.2	What kinds of ions do metals and non-metals form?	
4.3	What name is given to elements in group 0?	
4.4	Why are the group 0 elements unreactive?	
4.5	How does the boiling point of group 0 elements change down the group?	
4.6	Explain why the group 1 elements are called alkali metals	
4.7	What are the products of the alkali metals in a reaction with: oxygen, water, halogen?	
4.8	Explain why the group 1 elements get more reactive down the group	
4.9	What name is given to elements in group 7?	
4.10	How does the boiling point of group 7 elements change down the group?	
4.11	Explain why the group 7 elements get less reactive down the group	
4.12	What is a displacement reaction?	

Section 5: Bonding and Structure 1

ANSWER KEY

5.1	What are the three types of bond?	Covalent, ionic and metallic
5.2	What happens to the electrons in an ionic bond?	They are transferred
5.3	If an atom has gained electrons, what charge will it have as an ion?	Negative
5.4	If an atom has lost electrons, what charge will it have has an ion?	Positive
5.5	What type of elements will form ionic bonds?	Metal + non-metal
5.6	What is the charge on elements from group one and two?	Group 1: 1+, group 2: 2+
5.7	What is the charge on elements from group six and seven?	Group 6: 2-, group 7: 1-
5.8	Describe the structure and bonding in an ionic compound	Giant ionic lattice held together by strong electrostatic force of attraction between positive and negative ions
5.9	State the melting and boiling points of ionic compounds	High
5.10	Explain the melting and boiling points of ionic compounds	High due to strong electrostatic forces of attraction which require a lot of energy to break
5.11	Explain why ionic compounds do not conduct electricity when solid	The ions are not free to move and carry charge
5.12	Explain why ionic compounds conduct electricity when molten or in solution	The ions are free to move and carry charge

Section 5: Bonding and Structure 1

TRACKER

Quiz	Date	Score
1		
2		
3		
4		
5		
6		

Got it? ☐

5.1	What are the three types of bond?	
5.2	What happens to the electrons in an ionic bond?	
5.3	If an atom has gained electrons, what charge will it have as an ion?	
5.4	If an atom has lost electrons, what charge will it have has an ion?	
5.5	What type of elements will form ionic bonds?	
5.6	What is the charge on elements from group one and two?	
5.7	What is the charge on elements from group six and seven?	
5.8	Describe the structure and bonding in an ionic compound	
5.9	State the melting and boiling points of ionic compounds	
5.10	Explain the melting and boiling points of ionic compounds	
5.11	Explain why ionic compounds do not conduct electricity when solid	
5.12	Explain why ionic compounds conduct electricity when molten or in solution	

Section 5: Bonding and Structure 1

5.1	What are the three types of bond?	
5.2	What happens to the electrons in an ionic bond?	
5.3	If an atom has gained electrons, what charge will it have as an ion?	
5.4	If an atom has lost electrons, what charge will it have has an ion?	
5.5	What type of elements will form ionic bonds?	
5.6	What is the charge on elements from group one and two?	
5.7	What is the charge on elements from group six and seven?	
5.8	Describe the structure and bonding in an ionic compound	
5.9	State the melting and boiling points of ionic compounds	
5.10	Explain the melting and boiling points of ionic compounds	
5.11	Explain why ionic compounds do not conduct electricity when solid	
5.12	Explain why ionic compounds conduct electricity when molten or in solution	

5.1	What are the three types of bond?	
5.2	What happens to the electrons in an ionic bond?	
5.3	If an atom has gained electrons, what charge will it have as an ion?	
5.4	If an atom has lost electrons, what charge will it have has an ion?	
5.5	What type of elements will form ionic bonds?	
5.6	What is the charge on elements from group one and two?	
5.7	What is the charge on elements from group six and seven?	
5.8	Describe the structure and bonding in an ionic compound	
5.9	State the melting and boiling points of ionic compounds	
5.10	Explain the melting and boiling points of ionic compounds	
5.11	Explain why ionic compounds do not conduct electricity when solid	
5.12	Explain why ionic compounds conduct electricity when molten or in solution	

5.1	What are the three types of bond?	
5.2	What happens to the electrons in an ionic bond?	
5.3	If an atom has gained electrons, what charge will it have as an ion?	
5.4	If an atom has lost electrons, what charge will it have has an ion?	
5.5	What type of elements will form ionic bonds?	
5.6	What is the charge on elements from group one and two?	
5.7	What is the charge on elements from group six and seven?	
5.8	Describe the structure and bonding in an ionic compound	
5.9	State the melting and boiling points of ionic compounds	
5.10	Explain the melting and boiling points of ionic compounds	
5.11	Explain why ionic compounds do not conduct electricity when solid	
5.12	Explain why ionic compounds conduct electricity when molten or in solution	

Section 5: Bonding and Structure 1

5.1	What are the three types of bond?	
5.2	What happens to the electrons in an ionic bond?	
5.3	If an atom has gained electrons, what charge will it have as an ion?	
5.4	If an atom has lost electrons, what charge will it have has an ion?	
5.5	What type of elements will form ionic bonds?	
5.6	What is the charge on elements from group one and two?	
5.7	What is the charge on elements from group six and seven?	
5.8	Describe the structure and bonding in an ionic compound	
5.9	State the melting and boiling points of ionic compounds	
5.10	Explain the melting and boiling points of ionic compounds	
5.11	Explain why ionic compounds do not conduct electricity when solid	
5.12	Explain why ionic compounds conduct electricity when molten or in solution	

5.1	What are the three types of bond?	
5.2	What happens to the electrons in an ionic bond?	
5.3	If an atom has gained electrons, what charge will it have as an ion?	
5.4	If an atom has lost electrons, what charge will it have has an ion?	
5.5	What type of elements will form ionic bonds?	
5.6	What is the charge on elements from group one and two?	
5.7	What is the charge on elements from group six and seven?	
5.8	Describe the structure and bonding in an ionic compound	
5.9	State the melting and boiling points of ionic compounds	
5.10	Explain the melting and boiling points of ionic compounds	
5.11	Explain why ionic compounds do not conduct electricity when solid	
5.12	Explain why ionic compounds conduct electricity when molten or in solution	

Section 6: Bonding and Structure 2

ANSWER KEY

6.1	What happens to the electrons in a covalent bond?	They are shared
6.2	What type of elements will form covalent bonds?	Non-metal + non-metal
6.3	What two types of substance have covalent bonds?	Giant covalent substances and small molecules
6.4	How many bonds does each carbon have in diamond?	4
6.5	Explain why diamond and silicon dioxide have high melting points	Giant structures, strong covalent bonds between the atoms, requires a lot of energy to break
6.6	Explain why most covalent substances do not conduct electricity	There are no electrons or ions that are free to move and carry charge
6.7	Making full reference to structure and bonding in graphite, explain how it conducts electricity	Each carbon has 3 bonds, 1 electron is delocalised and therefore free to carry charge through the graphite
6.8	Explain why graphite can act as a lubricant	Weak forces between layers which are free to slide over each other
6.9	What type of substance are methane and water?	Small molecules
6.10	Describe the structure of small molecules	Strong covalent bonds between atoms, weak intermolecular forces holding the molecules together
6.11	Explain why small molecules have low melting points	It is a simple molecular substance with weak forces between the molecules (which are easy to break)
6.12	What is a polymer?	Millions of small molecules joined together in a chain to form a large molecule

TRACKER

Quiz	Date	Score
1		
2		
3		
4		
5		
6		

Got it? ☐

6.1	What happens to the electrons in a covalent bond?	
6.2	What type of elements will form covalent bonds?	
6.3	What two types of substance have covalent bonds?	
6.4	How many bonds does each carbon have in diamond?	
6.5	Explain why diamond and silicon dioxide have high melting points	
6.6	Explain why most covalent substances do not conduct electricity	
6.7	Making full reference to structure and bonding in graphite, explain how it conducts electricity	
6.8	Explain why graphite can act as a lubricant	
6.9	What type of substance are methane and water?	
6.10	Describe the structure of small molecules	
6.11	Explain why small molecules have low melting points	
6.12	What is a polymer?	

6.1	What happens to the electrons in a covalent bond?	
6.2	What type of elements will form covalent bonds?	
6.3	What two types of substance have covalent bonds?	
6.4	How many bonds does each carbon have in diamond?	
6.5	Explain why diamond and silicon dioxide have high melting points	
6.6	Explain why most covalent substances do not conduct electricity	
6.7	Making full reference to structure and bonding in graphite, explain how it conducts electricity	
6.8	Explain why graphite can act as a lubricant	
6.9	What type of substance are methane and water?	
6.10	Describe the structure of small molecules	
6.11	Explain why small molecules have low melting points	
6.12	What is a polymer?	

6.1	What happens to the electrons in a covalent bond?	
6.2	What type of elements will form covalent bonds?	
6.3	What two types of substance have covalent bonds?	
6.4	How many bonds does each carbon have in diamond?	
6.5	Explain why diamond and silicon dioxide have high melting points	
6.6	Explain why most covalent substances do not conduct electricity	
6.7	Making full reference to structure and bonding in graphite, explain how it conducts electricity	
6.8	Explain why graphite can act as a lubricant	
6.9	What type of substance are methane and water?	
6.10	Describe the structure of small molecules	
6.11	Explain why small molecules have low melting points	
6.12	What is a polymer?	

6.1	What happens to the electrons in a covalent bond?	
6.2	What type of elements will form covalent bonds?	
6.3	What two types of substance have covalent bonds?	
6.4	How many bonds does each carbon have in diamond?	
6.5	Explain why diamond and silicon dioxide have high melting points	
6.6	Explain why most covalent substances do not conduct electricity	
6.7	Making full reference to structure and bonding in graphite, explain how it conducts electricity	
6.8	Explain why graphite can act as a lubricant	
6.9	What type of substance are methane and water?	
6.10	Describe the structure of small molecules	
6.11	Explain why small molecules have low melting points	
6.12	What is a polymer?	

Section 6: Bonding and Structure 2

6.1	What happens to the electrons in a covalent bond?	
6.2	What type of elements will form covalent bonds?	
6.3	What two types of substance have covalent bonds?	
6.4	How many bonds does each carbon have in diamond?	
6.5	Explain why diamond and silicon dioxide have high melting points	
6.6	Explain why most covalent substances do not conduct electricity	
6.7	Making full reference to structure and bonding in graphite, explain how it conducts electricity	
6.8	Explain why graphite can act as a lubricant	
6.9	What type of substance are methane and water?	
6.10	Describe the structure of small molecules	
6.11	Explain why small molecules have low melting points	
6.12	What is a polymer?	

6.1	What happens to the electrons in a covalent bond?	
6.2	What type of elements will form covalent bonds?	
6.3	What two types of substance have covalent bonds?	
6.4	How many bonds does each carbon have in diamond?	
6.5	Explain why diamond and silicon dioxide have high melting points	
6.6	Explain why most covalent substances do not conduct electricity	
6.7	Making full reference to structure and bonding in graphite, explain how it conducts electricity	
6.8	Explain why graphite can act as a lubricant	
6.9	What type of substance are methane and water?	
6.10	Describe the structure of small molecules	
6.11	Explain why small molecules have low melting points	
6.12	What is a polymer?	

ANSWER KEY

7.1	Why do larger molecules have higher melting points than smaller ones?	Intermolecular force strengthens with increased molecule size
7.2	What is graphene?	One layer of graphite
7.3	What is graphene used for?	Electronics and composite materials
7.4	What is a fullerene?	Substance made of carbon atoms arranged in a cage
7.5	What are nanotubes?	Cylindrical fullerenes
7.6	What are nanotubes used for?	Electronics, nanotechnology and materials

TRACKER

Quiz	Date	Score
1		
2		
3		
4		
5		
6		

Got it? ☐

7.1	Why do larger molecules have higher melting points than smaller ones?	
7.2	What is graphene?	
7.3	What is graphene used for?	
7.4	What is a fullerene?	
7.5	What are nanotubes?	
7.6	What are nanotubes used for?	

7.1	Why do larger molecules have higher melting points than smaller ones?	
7.2	What is graphene?	
7.3	What is graphene used for?	
7.4	What is a fullerene?	
7.5	What are nanotubes?	
7.6	What are nanotubes used for?	

7.1	Why do larger molecules have higher melting points than smaller ones?	
7.2	What is graphene?	
7.3	What is graphene used for?	
7.4	What is a fullerene?	
7.5	What are nanotubes?	
7.6	What are nanotubes used for?	

7.1	Why do larger molecules have higher melting points than smaller ones?	
7.2	What is graphene?	
7.3	What is graphene used for?	
7.4	What is a fullerene?	
7.5	What are nanotubes?	
7.6	What are nanotubes used for?	

Section 7: Bonding and Structure 3

7.1	Why do larger molecules have higher melting points than smaller ones?	
7.2	What is graphene?	
7.3	What is graphene used for?	
7.4	What is a fullerene?	
7.5	What are nanotubes?	
7.6	What are nanotubes used for?	

7.1	Why do larger molecules have higher melting points than smaller ones?	
7.2	What is graphene?	
7.3	What is graphene used for?	
7.4	What is a fullerene?	
7.5	What are nanotubes?	
7.6	What are nanotubes used for?	

Section 8: Quantitative Chemistry

ANSWER KEY

8.1	What is the conservation of mass?	That atoms cannot be created or destroyed
8.2	When a metal forms a metal oxide, why does the mass increase?	Because oxygen atoms have been added
8.3	When an acid reacts with a metal, why does the mass decrease?	Because a gas is produced and escapes
8.4	What is relative formula mass?	The sum of the relative masses of each atom in a compound
8.5	What are the four state symbols and what do they stand for?	(s) solid (l) liquid (g) gas (aq) aqueous
8.6	What symbol do we use for relative formula mass?	Mr
8.7	(HT) What is a mole?	A number of particles
8.8	(HT) What is Avogadro's number?	6.022×10^{23}
8.9	(HT) What formula relates moles, mass and Mr?	Moles = mass/Mr
8.10	(HT) What is a limiting reactant?	A reactant that does not have enough mass to react with all the product
8.11	What is the unit for concentration?	g/dm^3
8.12	Which formula relates concentration, mass and volume?	concentration = mass/volume

TRACKER

Quiz	Date	Score
1		
2		
3		
4		
5		
6		

Got it? ☐

Section 8: Quantitative Chemistry

8.1	What is the conservation of mass?	
8.2	When a metal forms a metal oxide, why does the mass increase?	
8.3	When an acid reacts with a metal, why does the mass decrease?	
8.4	What is relative formula mass?	
8.5	What are the four state symbols and what do they stand for?	
8.6	What symbol do we use for relative formula mass?	
8.7	(HT) What is a mole?	
8.8	(HT) What is Avogadro's number?	
8.9	(HT) What formula relates moles, mass and Mr?	
8.10	(HT) What is a limiting reactant?	
8.11	What is the unit for concentration?	
8.12	Which formula relates concentration, mass and volume?	

Section 8: Quantitative Chemistry

8.1	What is the conservation of mass?	
8.2	When a metal forms a metal oxide, why does the mass increase?	
8.3	When an acid reacts with a metal, why does the mass decrease?	
8.4	What is relative formula mass?	
8.5	What are the four state symbols and what do they stand for?	
8.6	What symbol do we use for relative formula mass?	
8.7	(HT) What is a mole?	
8.8	(HT) What is Avogadro's number?	
8.9	(HT) What formula relates moles, mass and Mr?	
8.10	(HT) What is a limiting reactant?	
8.11	What is the unit for concentration?	
8.12	Which formula relates concentration, mass and volume?	

Section 8: Quantitative Chemistry

8.1	What is the conservation of mass?	
8.2	When a metal forms a metal oxide, why does the mass increase?	
8.3	When an acid reacts with a metal, why does the mass decrease?	
8.4	What is relative formula mass?	
8.5	What are the four state symbols and what do they stand for?	
8.6	What symbol do we use for relative formula mass?	
8.7	(HT) What is a mole?	
8.8	(HT) What is Avogadro's number?	
8.9	(HT) What formula relates moles, mass and Mr?	
8.10	(HT) What is a limiting reactant?	
8.11	What is the unit for concentration?	
8.12	Which formula relates concentration, mass and volume?	

Section 8: Quantitative Chemistry

8.1	What is the conservation of mass?	
8.2	When a metal forms a metal oxide, why does the mass increase?	
8.3	When an acid reacts with a metal, why does the mass decrease?	
8.4	What is relative formula mass?	
8.5	What are the four state symbols and what do they stand for?	
8.6	What symbol do we use for relative formula mass?	
8.7	(HT) What is a mole?	
8.8	(HT) What is Avogadro's number?	
8.9	(HT) What formula relates moles, mass and Mr?	
8.10	(HT) What is a limiting reactant?	
8.11	What is the unit for concentration?	
8.12	Which formula relates concentration, mass and volume?	

Section 8: Quantitative Chemistry

8.1	What is the conservation of mass?	
8.2	When a metal forms a metal oxide, why does the mass increase?	
8.3	When an acid reacts with a metal, why does the mass decrease?	
8.4	What is relative formula mass?	
8.5	What are the four state symbols and what do they stand for?	
8.6	What symbol do we use for relative formula mass?	
8.7	(HT) What is a mole?	
8.8	(HT) What is Avogadro's number?	
8.9	(HT) What formula relates moles, mass and Mr?	
8.10	(HT) What is a limiting reactant?	
8.11	What is the unit for concentration?	
8.12	Which formula relates concentration, mass and volume?	

Section 8: Quantitative Chemistry

8.1	What is the conservation of mass?	
8.2	When a metal forms a metal oxide, why does the mass increase?	
8.3	When an acid reacts with a metal, why does the mass decrease?	
8.4	What is relative formula mass?	
8.5	What are the four state symbols and what do they stand for?	
8.6	What symbol do we use for relative formula mass?	
8.7	(HT) What is a mole?	
8.8	(HT) What is Avogadro's number?	
8.9	(HT) What formula relates moles, mass and Mr?	
8.10	(HT) What is a limiting reactant?	
8.11	What is the unit for concentration?	
8.12	Which formula relates concentration, mass and volume?	

ANSWER KEY

9.1	What is the reactivity series?	A list of elements ordered by their reactivity
9.2	How can metals be placed in order of their reactivity?	Add the metals to water or acid and see which ones react the most vigorously
9.3	What is the name for a reaction where oxygen is removed from a compound?	Reduction
9.4	Why is gold found in the Earth's crust as the metal itself?	It is unreactive
9.5	What process is used to extract metals less reactive than carbon?	Reduction with carbon
9.6	What process is used to extract metals more reactive than carbon?	Electrolysis
9.7	What is an ore?	A material containing enough metal in it for it to be economically worthwhile to extract the metal.
9.8	What is a displacement reaction?	A reaction in which a more reactive element takes the place of a less reactive element in one of its compounds or in solution
9.9	Define oxidation in the context of loss and gain of electrons	Oxidation is the loss of electrons
9.10	Define reduction in the context of loss and gain of electrons	Reduction is the gain of electrons
9.11	Define acid in terms of pH	A substance with a pH of less than 7
9.12	Define acids in terms of ions	A substance which releases H^+ ions in solution
9.13	State the three common acids and give their formulae	Hydrochloric acid, $HCl(aq)$, Sulphuric acid, $H_2SO_4(aq)$, Nitric acid, HNO_3

TRACKER

Quiz	Date	Score
1		
2		
3		
4		
5		
6		

Got it? ☐

9.1	What is the reactivity series?	
9.2	How can metals be placed in order of their reactivity?	
9.3	What is the name for a reaction where oxygen is removed from a compound?	
9.4	Why is gold found in the Earth's crust as the metal itself?	
9.5	What process is used to extract metals less reactive than carbon?	
9.6	What process is used to extract metals more reactive than carbon?	
9.7	What is an ore?	
9.8	What is a displacement reaction?	
9.9	Define oxidation in the context of loss and gain of electrons	
9.10	Define reduction in the context of loss and gain of electrons	
9.11	Define acid in terms of pH	
9.12	Define acids in terms of ions	
9.13	State the three common acids and give their formulae	

9.1	What is the reactivity series?	
9.2	How can metals be placed in order of their reactivity?	
9.3	What is the name for a reaction where oxygen is removed from a compound?	
9.4	Why is gold found in the Earth's crust as the metal itself?	
9.5	What process is used to extract metals less reactive than carbon?	
9.6	What process is used to extract metals more reactive than carbon?	
9.7	What is an ore?	
9.8	What is a displacement reaction?	
9.9	Define oxidation in the context of loss and gain of electrons	
9.10	Define reduction in the context of loss and gain of electrons	
9.11	Define acid in terms of pH	
9.12	Define acids in terms of ions	
9.13	State the three common acids and give their formulae	

Section 9: Chemical Changes 1

9.1	What is the reactivity series?	
9.2	How can metals be placed in order of their reactivity?	
9.3	What is the name for a reaction where oxygen is removed from a compound?	
9.4	Why is gold found in the Earth's crust as the metal itself?	
9.5	What process is used to extract metals less reactive than carbon?	
9.6	What process is used to extract metals more reactive than carbon?	
9.7	What is an ore?	
9.8	What is a displacement reaction?	
9.9	Define oxidation in the context of loss and gain of electrons	
9.10	Define reduction in the context of loss and gain of electrons	
9.11	Define acid in terms of pH	
9.12	Define acids in terms of ions	
9.13	State the three common acids and give their formulae	

9.1	What is the reactivity series?	
9.2	How can metals be placed in order of their reactivity?	
9.3	What is the name for a reaction where oxygen is removed from a compound?	
9.4	Why is gold found in the Earth's crust as the metal itself?	
9.5	What process is used to extract metals less reactive than carbon?	
9.6	What process is used to extract metals more reactive than carbon?	
9.7	What is an ore?	
9.8	What is a displacement reaction?	
9.9	Define oxidation in the context of loss and gain of electrons	
9.10	Define reduction in the context of loss and gain of electrons	
9.11	Define acid in terms of pH	
9.12	Define acids in terms of ions	
9.13	State the three common acids and give their formulae	

9.1	What is the reactivity series?	
9.2	How can metals be placed in order of their reactivity?	
9.3	What is the name for a reaction where oxygen is removed from a compound?	
9.4	Why is gold found in the Earth's crust as the metal itself?	
9.5	What process is used to extract metals less reactive than carbon?	
9.6	What process is used to extract metals more reactive than carbon?	
9.7	What is an ore?	
9.8	What is a displacement reaction?	
9.9	Define oxidation in the context of loss and gain of electrons	
9.10	Define reduction in the context of loss and gain of electrons	
9.11	Define acid in terms of pH	
9.12	Define acids in terms of ions	
9.13	State the three common acids and give their formulae	

Section 9: Chemical Changes 1

9.1	What is the reactivity series?	
9.2	How can metals be placed in order of their reactivity?	
9.3	What is the name for a reaction where oxygen is removed from a compound?	
9.4	Why is gold found in the Earth's crust as the metal itself?	
9.5	What process is used to extract metals less reactive than carbon?	
9.6	What process is used to extract metals more reactive than carbon?	
9.7	What is an ore?	
9.8	What is a displacement reaction?	
9.9	Define oxidation in the context of loss and gain of electrons	
9.10	Define reduction in the context of loss and gain of electrons	
9.11	Define acid in terms of pH	
9.12	Define acids in terms of ions	
9.13	State the three common acids and give their formulae	

ANSWER KEY

10.1	Which ions do the common acids form in solution?	HCl forms H^+ and Cl^-, H_2SO_4 forms $2H^+$ and SO_4^{2-}, HNO_3 forms H^+ and NO_3^-
10.2	What is a neutral solution?	A solution with a pH of 7. Water is an example.
10.3	How do you measure pH?	With an indicator or pH probe.
10.4	What is a base?	A metal oxide, hydroxide or carbonate that will react with an acid. E.g. copper oxide
10.5	What is an alkali?	A soluble base. E.g. sodium hydroxide
10.6	Which ions are always present in a solution of an alkali?	OH^-
10.7	What is a salt?	A compound formed when some or all of the hydrogen from an acid is replaced by a metal.
10.8	What type of salts are formed by the three main acids?	Hydrochloric acid produces chlorides, sulphuric acid = sulphates, nitric acid = nitrates
10.9	What is a neutralisation reaction?	A reaction involving an acid that results in a neutral solution
10.10	Which ions always react together in a neutralization reactions between acids and alkalis?	H^+ and OH^-
10.11	Write the equation showing the reaction between H^+ and OH^- ions	$H^+ + OH^- \rightarrow H_2O$
10.12	Complete the equation: metal + acid $\rightarrow$	$\rightarrow$ salt + hydrogen gas
10.13	Complete the equation: metal hydroxide + acid $\rightarrow$	$\rightarrow$ salt + water

TRACKER

Quiz	Date	Score
1		
2		
3		
4		
5		
6		

Got it? ☐

10.1	Which ions do the common acids form in solution?	
10.2	What is a neutral solution?	
10.3	How do you measure pH?	
10.4	What is a base?	
10.5	What is an alkali?	
10.6	Which ions are always present in a solution of an alkali?	
10.7	What is a salt?	
10.8	What type of salts are formed by the three main acids?	
10.9	What is a neutralisation reaction?	
10.10	Which ions always react together in a neutralization reactions between acids and alkalis?	
10.11	Write the equation showing the reaction between H^+ and OH^- ions	
10.12	Complete the equation: metal + acid $\rightarrow$	
10.13	Complete the equation: metal hydroxide + acid $\rightarrow$	

10.1	Which ions do the common acids form in solution?	
10.2	What is a neutral solution?	
10.3	How do you measure pH?	
10.4	What is a base?	
10.5	What is an alkali?	
10.6	Which ions are always present in a solution of an alkali?	
10.7	What is a salt?	
10.8	What type of salts are formed by the three main acids?	
10.9	What is a neutralisation reaction?	
10.10	Which ions always react together in a neutralization reactions between acids and alkalis?	
10.11	Write the equation showing the reaction between H^+ and OH^- ions	
10.12	Complete the equation: metal + acid $\rightarrow$	
10.13	Complete the equation: metal hydroxide + acid $\rightarrow$	

10.1	Which ions do the common acids form in solution?	
10.2	What is a neutral solution?	
10.3	How do you measure pH?	
10.4	What is a base?	
10.5	What is an alkali?	
10.6	Which ions are always present in a solution of an alkali?	
10.7	What is a salt?	
10.8	What type of salts are formed by the three main acids?	
10.9	What is a neutralisation reaction?	
10.10	Which ions always react together in a neutralization reactions between acids and alkalis?	
10.11	Write the equation showing the reaction between H^+ and OH^- ions	
10.12	Complete the equation: metal + acid →	
10.13	Complete the equation: metal hydroxide + acid →	

10.1	Which ions do the common acids form in solution?	
10.2	What is a neutral solution?	
10.3	How do you measure pH?	
10.4	What is a base?	
10.5	What is an alkali?	
10.6	Which ions are always present in a solution of an alkali?	
10.7	What is a salt?	
10.8	What type of salts are formed by the three main acids?	
10.9	What is a neutralisation reaction?	
10.10	Which ions always react together in a neutralization reactions between acids and alkalis?	
10.11	Write the equation showing the reaction between H^+ and OH^- ions	
10.12	Complete the equation: metal + acid $\rightarrow$	
10.13	Complete the equation: metal hydroxide + acid $\rightarrow$	

10.1	Which ions do the common acids form in solution?	
10.2	What is a neutral solution?	
10.3	How do you measure pH?	
10.4	What is a base?	
10.5	What is an alkali?	
10.6	Which ions are always present in a solution of an alkali?	
10.7	What is a salt?	
10.8	What type of salts are formed by the three main acids?	
10.9	What is a neutralisation reaction?	
10.10	Which ions always react together in a neutralization reactions between acids and alkalis?	
10.11	Write the equation showing the reaction between H^+ and OH^- ions	
10.12	Complete the equation: metal + acid →	
10.13	Complete the equation: metal hydroxide + acid →	

Section 10: Chemical Changes 2

10.1	Which ions do the common acids form in solution?	
10.2	What is a neutral solution?	
10.3	How do you measure pH?	
10.4	What is a base?	
10.5	What is an alkali?	
10.6	Which ions are always present in a solution of an alkali?	
10.7	What is a salt?	
10.8	What type of salts are formed by the three main acids?	
10.9	What is a neutralisation reaction?	
10.10	Which ions always react together in a neutralization reactions between acids and alkalis?	
10.11	Write the equation showing the reaction between H^+ and OH^- ions	
10.12	Complete the equation: metal + acid $\rightarrow$	
10.13	Complete the equation: metal hydroxide + acid $\rightarrow$	

ANSWER KEY

11.1	Complete the equation: metal oxide + acid →	→ salt + water
11.2	Complete the equation: metal carbonate + acid →	→ salt + water + carbon dioxide
11.3	How do you make a soluble salt from an acid?	React the acid with a base. E.g. to make copper sulphate react copper oxide with sulphuric acid
11.4	If a salt is in solution, how do you extract it as a solid?	Allow the water to evaporate and it will leave the salt behind as a solid (crystallisation)
11.5	What is a strong acid?	An acid which completely splits up into its ions in water. E.g. when HCl is in water all the HCl molecules split up into H^+ and Cl^-
11.6	What is a weak acid?	An acid which will have some molecules which do not split up into their ions. E.g. in ethanoic acid only some of the molecules will have split up into the ethanoate ion and H^+ ions.
11.7	What is the relationship between the strength of an acid and its pH?	As an acid increases in strength the pH decreases.
11.8	What is a concentrated acid?	An acid where there are lots of acid particles in the water.
11.9	What is a dilute acid?	An acid where there are fewer acid particles in the water.
11.10	How does pH depend on the concentration of H^+ in a solution?	As the concentration of H^+ increases by a factor of ten, the pH decreases by one
11.11	What is electrolysis?	Using electricity to produce elements from an ionic compound
11.12	What is an electrolyte?	A liquid or aqueous ionic compound
11.13	What is the name for the positive electrode?	The anode

TRACKER

Quiz	Date	Score
1		
2		
3		
4		
5		
6		

Got it? ☐

11.1	Complete the equation: metal oxide + acid →	
11.2	Complete the equation: metal carbonate + acid →	
11.3	How do you make a soluble salt from an acid?	
11.4	If a salt is in solution, how do you extract it as a solid?	
11.5	What is a strong acid?	
11.6	What is a weak acid?	
11.7	What is the relationship between the strength of an acid and its pH?	
11.8	What is a concentrated acid?	
11.9	What is a dilute acid?	
11.10	How does pH depend on the concentration of H^+ in a solution?	
11.11	What is electrolysis?	
11.12	What is an electrolyte?	
11.13	What is the name for the positive electrode?	

Section 11: Chemical Changes 3

11.1	Complete the equation: metal oxide + acid →	
11.2	Complete the equation: metal carbonate + acid →	
11.3	How do you make a soluble salt from an acid?	
11.4	If a salt is in solution, how do you extract it as a solid?	
11.5	What is a strong acid?	
11.6	What is a weak acid?	
11.7	What is the relationship between the strength of an acid and its pH?	
11.8	What is a concentrated acid?	
11.9	What is a dilute acid?	
11.10	How does pH depend on the concentration of H^+ in a solution?	
11.11	What is electrolysis?	
11.12	What is an electrolyte?	
11.13	What is the name for the positive electrode?	

11.1	Complete the equation: metal oxide + acid →	
11.2	Complete the equation: metal carbonate + acid →	
11.3	How do you make a soluble salt from an acid?	
11.4	If a salt is in solution, how do you extract it as a solid?	
11.5	What is a strong acid?	
11.6	What is a weak acid?	
11.7	What is the relationship between the strength of an acid and its pH?	
11.8	What is a concentrated acid?	
11.9	What is a dilute acid?	
11.10	How does pH depend on the concentration of H^+ in a solution?	
11.11	What is electrolysis?	
11.12	What is an electrolyte?	
11.13	What is the name for the positive electrode?	

Section 11: Chemical Changes 3

11.1	Complete the equation: metal oxide + acid →	
11.2	Complete the equation: metal carbonate + acid →	
11.3	How do you make a soluble salt from an acid?	
11.4	If a salt is in solution, how do you extract it as a solid?	
11.5	What is a strong acid?	
11.6	What is a weak acid?	
11.7	What is the relationship between the strength of an acid and its pH?	
11.8	What is a concentrated acid?	
11.9	What is a dilute acid?	
11.10	How does pH depend on the concentration of H^+ in a solution?	
11.11	What is electrolysis?	
11.12	What is an electrolyte?	
11.13	What is the name for the positive electrode?	

11.1	Complete the equation: metal oxide + acid →	
11.2	Complete the equation: metal carbonate + acid →	
11.3	How do you make a soluble salt from an acid?	
11.4	If a salt is in solution, how do you extract it as a solid?	
11.5	What is a strong acid?	
11.6	What is a weak acid?	
11.7	What is the relationship between the strength of an acid and its pH?	
11.8	What is a concentrated acid?	
11.9	What is a dilute acid?	
11.10	How does pH depend on the concentration of H^+ in a solution?	
11.11	What is electrolysis?	
11.12	What is an electrolyte?	
11.13	What is the name for the positive electrode?	

11.1	Complete the equation: metal oxide + acid →	
11.2	Complete the equation: metal carbonate + acid →	
11.3	How do you make a soluble salt from an acid?	
11.4	If a salt is in solution, how do you extract it as a solid?	
11.5	What is a strong acid?	
11.6	What is a weak acid?	
11.7	What is the relationship between the strength of an acid and its pH?	
11.8	What is a concentrated acid?	
11.9	What is a dilute acid?	
11.10	How does pH depend on the concentration of H^+ in a solution?	
11.11	What is electrolysis?	
11.12	What is an electrolyte?	
11.13	What is the name for the positive electrode?	

ANSWER KEY

12.1	What is the name for the negative electrode?	The cathode
12.2	Do positive ions move to the anode or the cathode?	Cathode
12.3	Do negative ions move to the anode or the cathode?	Anode
12.4	What are the two main disadvantages of using electrolysis to extract metals?	Requires a large amount of energy to melt the compounds and to produce the necessary electricity
12.5	Why is aluminium oxide mixed with cryolite when extracting aluminium?	To lower the melting point
12.6	What is produced at the anode and cathode in the electrolysis of aluminium oxide?	Aluminium at the cathode and oxygen at the anode
12.7	Why does the anode need to be replaced in the electrolysis of aluminium oxide?	The oxygen reacts with the carbon electrode to produce carbon dioxide.
12.8	For a simple ionic liquid, where is the metal produced?	Cathode
12.9	For a simple ionic liquid, where is the non-metal produced?	Anode
12.10	In the electrolysis of an ionic solution, when will hydrogen be produced?	If it is more reactive than hydrogen
12.11	In the electrolysis of an ionic solution, when will oxygen be produced?	If the non-metal is not a halogen
12.12	What can happen to water molecules in the electrolysis of solutions?	They break down into hydrogen and hydroxide ions
12.13	What is a half equation?	An equation which shows electron transfer at one of the electrodes

TRACKER

Quiz	Date	Score
1		
2		
3		
4		
5		
6		

Got it? ☐

12.1	What is the name for the negative electrode?	
12.2	Do positive ions move to the anode or the cathode?	
12.3	Do negative ions move to the anode or the cathode?	
12.4	What are the two main disadvantages of using electrolysis to extract metals?	
12.5	Why is aluminium oxide mixed with cryolite when extracting aluminium?	
12.6	What is produced at the anode and cathode in the electrolysis of aluminium oxide?	
12.7	Why does the anode need to be replaced in the electrolysis of aluminium oxide?	
12.8	For a simple ionic liquid, where is the metal produced?	
12.9	For a simple ionic liquid, where is the non-metal produced?	
12.10	In the electrolysis of an ionic solution, when will hydrogen be produced?	
12.11	In the electrolysis of an ionic solution, when will oxygen be produced?	
12.12	What can happen to water molecules in the electrolysis of solutions?	
12.13	What is a half equation?	

12.1	What is the name for the negative electrode?	
12.2	Do positive ions move to the anode or the cathode?	
12.3	Do negative ions move to the anode or the cathode?	
12.4	What are the two main disadvantages of using electrolysis to extract metals?	
12.5	Why is aluminium oxide mixed with cryolite when extracting aluminium?	
12.6	What is produced at the anode and cathode in the electrolysis of aluminium oxide?	
12.7	Why does the anode need to be replaced in the electrolysis of aluminium oxide?	
12.8	For a simple ionic liquid, where is the metal produced?	
12.9	For a simple ionic liquid, where is the non-metal produced?	
12.10	In the electrolysis of an ionic solution, when will hydrogen be produced?	
12.11	In the electrolysis of an ionic solution, when will oxygen be produced?	
12.12	What can happen to water molecules in the electrolysis of solutions?	
12.13	What is a half equation?	

Section 12: Chemical Changes 4

12.1	What is the name for the negative electrode?	
12.2	Do positive ions move to the anode or the cathode?	
12.3	Do negative ions move to the anode or the cathode?	
12.4	What are the two main disadvantages of using electrolysis to extract metals?	
12.5	Why is aluminium oxide mixed with cryolite when extracting aluminium?	
12.6	What is produced at the anode and cathode in the electrolysis of aluminium oxide?	
12.7	Why does the anode need to be replaced in the electrolysis of aluminium oxide?	
12.8	For a simple ionic liquid, where is the metal produced?	
12.9	For a simple ionic liquid, where is the non-metal produced?	
12.10	In the electrolysis of an ionic solution, when will hydrogen be produced?	
12.11	In the electrolysis of an ionic solution, when will oxygen be produced?	
12.12	What can happen to water molecules in the electrolysis of solutions?	
12.13	What is a half equation?	

12.1	What is the name for the negative electrode?	
12.2	Do positive ions move to the anode or the cathode?	
12.3	Do negative ions move to the anode or the cathode?	
12.4	What are the two main disadvantages of using electrolysis to extract metals?	
12.5	Why is aluminium oxide mixed with cryolite when extracting aluminium?	
12.6	What is produced at the anode and cathode in the electrolysis of aluminium oxide?	
12.7	Why does the anode need to be replaced in the electrolysis of aluminium oxide?	
12.8	For a simple ionic liquid, where is the metal produced?	
12.9	For a simple ionic liquid, where is the non-metal produced?	
12.10	In the electrolysis of an ionic solution, when will hydrogen be produced?	
12.11	In the electrolysis of an ionic solution, when will oxygen be produced?	
12.12	What can happen to water molecules in the electrolysis of solutions?	
12.13	What is a half equation?	

12.1	What is the name for the negative electrode?	
12.2	Do positive ions move to the anode or the cathode?	
12.3	Do negative ions move to the anode or the cathode?	
12.4	What are the two main disadvantages of using electrolysis to extract metals?	
12.5	Why is aluminium oxide mixed with cryolite when extracting aluminium?	
12.6	What is produced at the anode and cathode in the electrolysis of aluminium oxide?	
12.7	Why does the anode need to be replaced in the electrolysis of aluminium oxide?	
12.8	For a simple ionic liquid, where is the metal produced?	
12.9	For a simple ionic liquid, where is the non-metal produced?	
12.10	In the electrolysis of an ionic solution, when will hydrogen be produced?	
12.11	In the electrolysis of an ionic solution, when will oxygen be produced?	
12.12	What can happen to water molecules in the electrolysis of solutions?	
12.13	What is a half equation?	

12.1	What is the name for the negative electrode?	
12.2	Do positive ions move to the anode or the cathode?	
12.3	Do negative ions move to the anode or the cathode?	
12.4	What are the two main disadvantages of using electrolysis to extract metals?	
12.5	Why is aluminium oxide mixed with cryolite when extracting aluminium?	
12.6	What is produced at the anode and cathode in the electrolysis of aluminium oxide?	
12.7	Why does the anode need to be replaced in the electrolysis of aluminium oxide?	
12.8	For a simple ionic liquid, where is the metal produced?	
12.9	For a simple ionic liquid, where is the non-metal produced?	
12.10	In the electrolysis of an ionic solution, when will hydrogen be produced?	
12.11	In the electrolysis of an ionic solution, when will oxygen be produced?	
12.12	What can happen to water molecules in the electrolysis of solutions?	
12.13	What is a half equation?	

Section 13: Energy Changes

ANSWER KEY

13.1	State the law of conservation of energy.	Energy cannot be created or destroyed, it can only transferred from one place to another.
13.2	What is an exothermic reaction?	A reaction where energy is transferred to the surroundings.
13.3	Give two examples of exothermic reactions.	Combustion, respiration
13.4	What happens to the temperature of the surroundings during an exothermic reaction?	Increases
13.5	What is an endothermic reaction?	A reaction where energy is transferred from the surroundings.
13.6	Give two examples of endothermic reactions.	Thermal decomposition reactions, citric acid and sodium hydrogencarbonate.
13.7	What happens to the temperature of the surroundings during an endothermic reaction?	Decreases
13.8	State two uses of exothermic reactions	Self-heating cans, hand warmers
13.9	State two uses of endothermic reactions	Some cooling sports injury packs
13.10	What is a reaction profile?	A diagram which shows whether the reactants have more or less energy than the products.
13.11	(HT) State which of bond breaking and bond making is endothermic and which is exothermic	Breaking: exothermic, making: endothermic
13.12	(HT) How do we work out the overall energy change of a reaction?	Work out the difference between the energy needed to break all the bonds in the reactants and the energy released to form all the bonds in the products.

TRACKER

Quiz	Date	Score
1		
2		
3		
4		
5		
6		

Got it? ☐

Section 13: Energy Changes

13.1	State the law of conservation of energy.	
13.2	What is an exothermic reaction?	
13.3	Give two examples of exothermic reactions.	
13.4	What happens to the temperature of the surroundings during an exothermic reaction?	
13.5	What is an endothermic reaction?	
13.6	Give two examples of endothermic reactions.	
13.7	What happens to the temperature of the surroundings during an endothermic reaction?	
13.8	State two uses of exothermic reactions	
13.9	State two uses of endothermic reactions	
13.10	What is a reaction profile?	
13.11	(HT) State which of bond breaking and bond making is endothermic and which is exothermic	
13.12	(HT) How do we work out the overall energy change of a reaction?	

Section 13: Energy Changes

13.1	State the law of conservation of energy.	
13.2	What is an exothermic reaction?	
13.3	Give two examples of exothermic reactions.	
13.4	What happens to the temperature of the surroundings during an exothermic reaction?	
13.5	What is an endothermic reaction?	
13.6	Give two examples of endothermic reactions.	
13.7	What happens to the temperature of the surroundings during an endothermic reaction?	
13.8	State two uses of exothermic reactions	
13.9	State two uses of endothermic reactions	
13.10	What is a reaction profile?	
13.11	(HT) State which of bond breaking and bond making is endothermic and which is exothermic	
13.12	(HT) How do we work out the overall energy change of a reaction?	

13.1	State the law of conservation of energy.	
13.2	What is an exothermic reaction?	
13.3	Give two examples of exothermic reactions.	
13.4	What happens to the temperature of the surroundings during an exothermic reaction?	
13.5	What is an endothermic reaction?	
13.6	Give two examples of endothermic reactions.	
13.7	What happens to the temperature of the surroundings during an endothermic reaction?	
13.8	State two uses of exothermic reactions	
13.9	State two uses of endothermic reactions	
13.10	What is a reaction profile?	
13.11	(HT) State which of bond breaking and bond making is endothermic and which is exothermic	
13.12	(HT) How do we work out the overall energy change of a reaction?	

Section 13: Energy Changes

13.1	State the law of conservation of energy.	
13.2	What is an exothermic reaction?	
13.3	Give two examples of exothermic reactions.	
13.4	What happens to the temperature of the surroundings during an exothermic reaction?	
13.5	What is an endothermic reaction?	
13.6	Give two examples of endothermic reactions.	
13.7	What happens to the temperature of the surroundings during an endothermic reaction?	
13.8	State two uses of exothermic reactions	
13.9	State two uses of endothermic reactions	
13.10	What is a reaction profile?	
13.11	(HT) State which of bond breaking and bond making is endothermic and which is exothermic	
13.12	(HT) How do we work out the overall energy change of a reaction?	

Section 13: Energy Changes

13.1	State the law of conservation of energy.	
13.2	What is an exothermic reaction?	
13.3	Give two examples of exothermic reactions.	
13.4	What happens to the temperature of the surroundings during an exothermic reaction?	
13.5	What is an endothermic reaction?	
13.6	Give two examples of endothermic reactions.	
13.7	What happens to the temperature of the surroundings during an endothermic reaction?	
13.8	State two uses of exothermic reactions	
13.9	State two uses of endothermic reactions	
13.10	What is a reaction profile?	
13.11	(HT) State which of bond breaking and bond making is endothermic and which is exothermic	
13.12	(HT) How do we work out the overall energy change of a reaction?	

13.1	State the law of conservation of energy.	
13.2	What is an exothermic reaction?	
13.3	Give two examples of exothermic reactions.	
13.4	What happens to the temperature of the surroundings during an exothermic reaction?	
13.5	What is an endothermic reaction?	
13.6	Give two examples of endothermic reactions.	
13.7	What happens to the temperature of the surroundings during an endothermic reaction?	
13.8	State two uses of exothermic reactions	
13.9	State two uses of endothermic reactions	
13.10	What is a reaction profile?	
13.11	(HT) State which of bond breaking and bond making is endothermic and which is exothermic	
13.12	(HT) How do we work out the overall energy change of a reaction?	

Section 14: Rate of Reaction 1

ANSWER KEY

14.1	What is the formula for a mean rate of reaction in terms of reactants?	quantity of reactant used/time taken
14.2	What is the formula for a mean rate of reaction in terms of products?	quantity of reactant product formed/time taken
14.3	How can you measure the quantity of a reactant or product?	In grams or in cm^3
14.4	What are the two possible units for rate of reaction?	g/s or cm^3/s (where s is seconds)
14.5	How could you measure the rate of a reaction from a graph?	Draw a tangent to the curve and calculate the gradient.
14.6	What is "collision theory"?	The theory that chemical reactions only occur when particles collide with sufficient energy
14.7	What five factors can affect the rate of a reaction?	Temperature, surface area of a solid, concentration of reactants in solution, pressure of gases, catalyst
14.8	State the effect of increasing the surface area on the rate of a reaction	Increases the rate
14.9	Explain why increasing the surface area increases the rate of a reaction	More particles are available to collide, there are therefore more frequent collisions between reactants.
14.10	State the effect of increasing the concentration on the rate of reaction	Increases
14.11	Explain why increasing the concentration increases the rate of reaction	More concentrated means more particles in solution, therefore more frequent collisions between reactants.
14.12	State the effect on increasing the pressure of a gas on the rate of reaction	Increases

TRACKER

Quiz	Date	Score
1		
2		
3		
4		
5		
6		

Got it? ☐

14.1	What is the formula for a mean rate of reaction in terms of reactants?	
14.2	What is the formula for a mean rate of reaction in terms of products?	
14.3	How can you measure the quantity of a reactant or product?	
14.4	What are the two possible units for rate of reaction?	
14.5	How could you measure the rate of a reaction from a graph?	
14.6	What is "collision theory"?	
14.7	What five factors can affect the rate of a reaction?	
14.8	State the effect of increasing the surface area on the rate of a reaction	
14.9	Explain why increasing the surface area increases the rate of a reaction	
14.10	State the effect of increasing the concentration on the rate of reaction	
14.11	Explain why increasing the concentration increases the rate of reaction	
14.12	State the effect on increasing the pressure of a gas on the rate of reaction	

14.1	What is the formula for a mean rate of reaction in terms of reactants?	
14.2	What is the formula for a mean rate of reaction in terms of products?	
14.3	How can you measure the quantity of a reactant or product?	
14.4	What are the two possible units for rate of reaction?	
14.5	How could you measure the rate of a reaction from a graph?	
14.6	What is "collision theory"?	
14.7	What five factors can affect the rate of a reaction?	
14.8	State the effect of increasing the surface area on the rate of a reaction	
14.9	Explain why increasing the surface area increases the rate of a reaction	
14.10	State the effect of increasing the concentration on the rate of reaction	
14.11	Explain why increasing the concentration increases the rate of reaction	
14.12	State the effect on increasing the pressure of a gas on the rate of reaction	

14.1	What is the formula for a mean rate of reaction in terms of reactants?	
14.2	What is the formula for a mean rate of reaction in terms of products?	
14.3	How can you measure the quantity of a reactant or product?	
14.4	What are the two possible units for rate of reaction?	
14.5	How could you measure the rate of a reaction from a graph?	
14.6	What is "collision theory"?	
14.7	What five factors can affect the rate of a reaction?	
14.8	State the effect of increasing the surface area on the rate of a reaction	
14.9	Explain why increasing the surface area increases the rate of a reaction	
14.10	State the effect of increasing the concentration on the rate of reaction	
14.11	Explain why increasing the concentration increases the rate of reaction	
14.12	State the effect on increasing the pressure of a gas on the rate of reaction	

14.1	What is the formula for a mean rate of reaction in terms of reactants?	
14.2	What is the formula for a mean rate of reaction in terms of products?	
14.3	How can you measure the quantity of a reactant or product?	
14.4	What are the two possible units for rate of reaction?	
14.5	How could you measure the rate of a reaction from a graph?	
14.6	What is "collision theory"?	
14.7	What five factors can affect the rate of a reaction?	
14.8	State the effect of increasing the surface area on the rate of a reaction	
14.9	Explain why increasing the surface area increases the rate of a reaction	
14.10	State the effect of increasing the concentration on the rate of reaction	
14.11	Explain why increasing the concentration increases the rate of reaction	
14.12	State the effect on increasing the pressure of a gas on the rate of reaction	

14.1	What is the formula for a mean rate of reaction in terms of reactants?	
14.2	What is the formula for a mean rate of reaction in terms of products?	
14.3	How can you measure the quantity of a reactant or product?	
14.4	What are the two possible units for rate of reaction?	
14.5	How could you measure the rate of a reaction from a graph?	
14.6	What is "collision theory"?	
14.7	What five factors can affect the rate of a reaction?	
14.8	State the effect of increasing the surface area on the rate of a reaction	
14.9	Explain why increasing the surface area increases the rate of a reaction	
14.10	State the effect of increasing the concentration on the rate of reaction	
14.11	Explain why increasing the concentration increases the rate of reaction	
14.12	State the effect on increasing the pressure of a gas on the rate of reaction	

14.1	What is the formula for a mean rate of reaction in terms of reactants?	
14.2	What is the formula for a mean rate of reaction in terms of products?	
14.3	How can you measure the quantity of a reactant or product?	
14.4	What are the two possible units for rate of reaction?	
14.5	How could you measure the rate of a reaction from a graph?	
14.6	What is "collision theory"?	
14.7	What five factors can affect the rate of a reaction?	
14.8	State the effect of increasing the surface area on the rate of a reaction	
14.9	Explain why increasing the surface area increases the rate of a reaction	
14.10	State the effect of increasing the concentration on the rate of reaction	
14.11	Explain why increasing the concentration increases the rate of reaction	
14.12	State the effect on increasing the pressure of a gas on the rate of reaction	

Section 15: Rate of Reaction 2

ANSWER KEY

15.1	Explain why increasing the pressure of a gas increases the rate of a reaction	Less space for the particles to move around in, therefore more frequent collisions
15.2	State the effect of increasing the temperature on the rate of reaction	Increases
15.3	What is the activation energy?	The amount of energy a particle needs before it will be able to react when it collides with another particle
15.4	Explain why increasing the temperature increases the rate of reaction	Increases the speed at which particles move therefore more frequent collisions. Increases the number of particles which have the activation energy therefore more collisions result in a reaction.
15.5	What is a catalyst?	Something which changes the rate of a reaction but is not used up in that reaction
15.6	How do catalysts speed up reactions?	They provide another route for the reaction to take place which has a lower activation energy.

TRACKER

Quiz	Date	Score
1		
2		
3		
4		
5		
6		

Got it? ☐

15.1	Explain why increasing the pressure of a gas increases the rate of a reaction	
15.2	State the effect of increasing the temperature on the rate of reaction	
15.3	What is the activation energy?	
15.4	Explain why increasing the temperature increases the rate of reaction	
15.5	What is a catalyst?	
15.6	How do catalysts speed up reactions?	

15.1	Explain why increasing the pressure of a gas increases the rate of a reaction	
15.2	State the effect of increasing the temperature on the rate of reaction	
15.3	What is the activation energy?	
15.4	Explain why increasing the temperature increases the rate of reaction	
15.5	What is a catalyst?	
15.6	How do catalysts speed up reactions?	

15.1	Explain why increasing the pressure of a gas increases the rate of a reaction	
15.2	State the effect of increasing the temperature on the rate of reaction	
15.3	What is the activation energy?	
15.4	Explain why increasing the temperature increases the rate of reaction	
15.5	What is a catalyst?	
15.6	How do catalysts speed up reactions?	

15.1	Explain why increasing the pressure of a gas increases the rate of a reaction	
15.2	State the effect of increasing the temperature on the rate of reaction	
15.3	What is the activation energy?	
15.4	Explain why increasing the temperature increases the rate of reaction	
15.5	What is a catalyst?	
15.6	How do catalysts speed up reactions?	

15.1	Explain why increasing the pressure of a gas increases the rate of a reaction	
15.2	State the effect of increasing the temperature on the rate of reaction	
15.3	What is the activation energy?	
15.4	Explain why increasing the temperature increases the rate of reaction	
15.5	What is a catalyst?	
15.6	How do catalysts speed up reactions?	

Section 15: Rate of Reaction 2

15.1	Explain why increasing the pressure of a gas increases the rate of a reaction	
15.2	State the effect of increasing the temperature on the rate of reaction	
15.3	What is the activation energy?	
15.4	Explain why increasing the temperature increases the rate of reaction	
15.5	What is a catalyst?	
15.6	How do catalysts speed up reactions?	

ANSWER KEY

16.1	What is a reversible reaction?	A reaction which can go from reactants to products but also from products to reactants
16.2	What chemical symbol represents a reversible reaction?	$\rightleftharpoons$
16.3	If a reaction is exothermic in the forward direction what will it be in the reverse direction?	Endothermic
16.4	What is dynamic equilibrium?	The point in a reversible reaction when the forward and reverse reactions are occurring at the same rate
16.5	How is the amount of reactant changing at equilibrium?	It is not changing
16.6	How is the amount of product changing at equilibrium?	It is not changing
16.7	(HT) What is Le Chatelier's principle?	When a reaction at equilibrium is changed, it will seek to counteract that change
16.8	(HT) A reaction is exothermic in the forward direction. What will occur if the temperature is increased?	The backward reaction will increase as it is endothermic and will reduce the temperature
16.9	(HT) A reaction is at equilibrium when some product is removed. What will occur?	The forward reaction will increase as that will increase the amount of product
16.10	(HT) How does increasing the pressure affect equilibrium?	Favours the side with fewer gaseous molecules

Section 16: Reversible Reactions

TRACKER

Quiz	Date	Score
1		
2		
3		
4		
5		
6		

Got it? ☐

Section 16: Reversible Reactions

16.1	What is a reversible reaction?	
16.2	What chemical symbol represents a reversible reaction?	
16.3	If a reaction is exothermic in the forward direction what will it be in the reverse direction?	
16.4	What is dynamic equilibrium?	
16.5	How is the amount of reactant changing at equilibrium?	
16.6	How is the amount of product changing at equilibrium?	
16.7	(HT) What is Le Chatelier's principle?	
16.8	(HT) A reaction is exothermic in the forward direction. What will occur if the temperature is increased?	
16.9	(HT) A reaction is at equilibrium when some product is removed. What will occur?	
16.10	(HT) How does increasing the pressure affect equilibrium?	

16.1	What is a reversible reaction?	
16.2	What chemical symbol represents a reversible reaction?	
16.3	If a reaction is exothermic in the forward direction what will it be in the reverse direction?	
16.4	What is dynamic equilibrium?	
16.5	How is the amount of reactant changing at equilibrium?	
16.6	How is the amount of product changing at equilibrium?	
16.7	(HT) What is Le Chatelier's principle?	
16.8	(HT) A reaction is exothermic in the forward direction. What will occur if the temperature is increased?	
16.9	(HT) A reaction is at equilibrium when some product is removed. What will occur?	
16.10	(HT) How does increasing the pressure affect equilibrium?	

16.1	What is a reversible reaction?	
16.2	What chemical symbol represents a reversible reaction?	
16.3	If a reaction is exothermic in the forward direction what will it be in the reverse direction?	
16.4	What is dynamic equilibrium?	
16.5	How is the amount of reactant changing at equilibrium?	
16.6	How is the amount of product changing at equilibrium?	
16.7	(HT) What is Le Chatelier's principle?	
16.8	(HT) A reaction is exothermic in the forward direction. What will occur if the temperature is increased?	
16.9	(HT) A reaction is at equilibrium when some product is removed. What will occur?	
16.10	(HT) How does increasing the pressure affect equilibrium?	

16.1	What is a reversible reaction?	
16.2	What chemical symbol represents a reversible reaction?	
16.3	If a reaction is exothermic in the forward direction what will it be in the reverse direction?	
16.4	What is dynamic equilibrium?	
16.5	How is the amount of reactant changing at equilibrium?	
16.6	How is the amount of product changing at equilibrium?	
16.7	(HT) What is Le Chatelier's principle?	
16.8	(HT) A reaction is exothermic in the forward direction. What will occur if the temperature is increased?	
16.9	(HT) A reaction is at equilibrium when some product is removed. What will occur?	
16.10	(HT) How does increasing the pressure affect equilibrium?	

Section 16: Reversible Reactions

16.1	What is a reversible reaction?	
16.2	What chemical symbol represents a reversible reaction?	
16.3	If a reaction is exothermic in the forward direction what will it be in the reverse direction?	
16.4	What is dynamic equilibrium?	
16.5	How is the amount of reactant changing at equilibrium?	
16.6	How is the amount of product changing at equilibrium?	
16.7	(HT) What is Le Chatelier's principle?	
16.8	(HT) A reaction is exothermic in the forward direction. What will occur if the temperature is increased?	
16.9	(HT) A reaction is at equilibrium when some product is removed. What will occur?	
16.10	(HT) How does increasing the pressure affect equilibrium?	

16.1	What is a reversible reaction?	
16.2	What chemical symbol represents a reversible reaction?	
16.3	If a reaction is exothermic in the forward direction what will it be in the reverse direction?	
16.4	What is dynamic equilibrium?	
16.5	How is the amount of reactant changing at equilibrium?	
16.6	How is the amount of product changing at equilibrium?	
16.7	(HT) What is Le Chatelier's principle?	
16.8	(HT) A reaction is exothermic in the forward direction. What will occur if the temperature is increased?	
16.9	(HT) A reaction is at equilibrium when some product is removed. What will occur?	
16.10	(HT) How does increasing the pressure affect equilibrium?	

Section 17: Organic Chemistry 1

ANSWER KEY

17.1	What is crude oil?	A mixture of hydrocarbons
17.2	What is crude oil formed from?	The remains of ancient biomass (mostly plankton) that was buried in mud
17.3	What is a finite resource?	One that will run out
17.4	Why is crude oil a finite resource?	Because it takes longer to form than the rate at which we are using it up
17.5	What is a hydrocarbon?	A compound made of atoms of carbon and hydrogen only
17.6	What is a general formula?	A mathematical formula which allows you to work out the chemical formula of a substance
17.7	What is an alkane?	A hydrocarbon with only single bonds
17.8	Name the first four alkanes	Methane, ethane, propane, butane
17.9	What is the general formula for alkanes?	$C_nH_{2n}+_2$
17.10	How does boiling point change with the length of an alkane?	The longer the alkane, the higher its boiling point
17.11	How does viscosity change with the length of an alkane?	The longer the alkane, the more viscous (the thicker) it is
17.12	How does flammability change with the length of an alkane?	The longer the alkane, the less flammable it is
17.13	What is fractional distillation?	A process used to separate mixtures of substances with different boiling points
17.14	What are the steps involved in fractional distillation?	Crude oil is vaporised, different molecules rise up the fractionating column and cool down. Condense at different points on the column.

TRACKER

Quiz	Date	Score
1		
2		
3		
4		
5		
6		

Got it? ☐

17.1	What is crude oil?	
17.2	What is crude oil formed from?	
17.3	What is a finite resource?	
17.4	Why is crude oil a finite resource?	
17.5	What is a hydrocarbon?	
17.6	What is a general formula?	
17.7	What is an alkane?	
17.8	Name the first four alkanes	
17.9	What is the general formula for alkanes?	
17.10	How does boiling point change with the length of an alkane?	
17.11	How does viscosity change with the length of an alkane?	
17.12	How does flammability change with the length of an alkane?	
17.13	What is fractional distillation?	
17.14	What are the steps involved in fractional distillation?	

Section 17: Organic Chemistry 1

17.1	What is crude oil?	
17.2	What is crude oil formed from?	
17.3	What is a finite resource?	
17.4	Why is crude oil a finite resource?	
17.5	What is a hydrocarbon?	
17.6	What is a general formula?	
17.7	What is an alkane?	
17.8	Name the first four alkanes	
17.9	What is the general formula for alkanes?	
17.10	How does boiling point change with the length of an alkane?	
17.11	How does viscosity change with the length of an alkane?	
17.12	How does flammability change with the length of an alkane?	
17.13	What is fractional distillation?	
17.14	What are the steps involved in fractional distillation?	

17.1	What is crude oil?	
17.2	What is crude oil formed from?	
17.3	What is a finite resource?	
17.4	Why is crude oil a finite resource?	
17.5	What is a hydrocarbon?	
17.6	What is a general formula?	
17.7	What is an alkane?	
17.8	Name the first four alkanes	
17.9	What is the general formula for alkanes?	
17.10	How does boiling point change with the length of an alkane?	
17.11	How does viscosity change with the length of an alkane?	
17.12	How does flammability change with the length of an alkane?	
17.13	What is fractional distillation?	
17.14	What are the steps involved in fractional distillation?	

17.1	What is crude oil?	
17.2	What is crude oil formed from?	
17.3	What is a finite resource?	
17.4	Why is crude oil a finite resource?	
17.5	What is a hydrocarbon?	
17.6	What is a general formula?	
17.7	What is an alkane?	
17.8	Name the first four alkanes	
17.9	What is the general formula for alkanes?	
17.10	How does boiling point change with the length of an alkane?	
17.11	How does viscosity change with the length of an alkane?	
17.12	How does flammability change with the length of an alkane?	
17.13	What is fractional distillation?	
17.14	What are the steps involved in fractional distillation?	

17.1	What is crude oil?	
17.2	What is crude oil formed from?	
17.3	What is a finite resource?	
17.4	Why is crude oil a finite resource?	
17.5	What is a hydrocarbon?	
17.6	What is a general formula?	
17.7	What is an alkane?	
17.8	Name the first four alkanes	
17.9	What is the general formula for alkanes?	
17.10	How does boiling point change with the length of an alkane?	
17.11	How does viscosity change with the length of an alkane?	
17.12	How does flammability change with the length of an alkane?	
17.13	What is fractional distillation?	
17.14	What are the steps involved in fractional distillation?	

17.1	What is crude oil?	
17.2	What is crude oil formed from?	
17.3	What is a finite resource?	
17.4	Why is crude oil a finite resource?	
17.5	What is a hydrocarbon?	
17.6	What is a general formula?	
17.7	What is an alkane?	
17.8	Name the first four alkanes	
17.9	What is the general formula for alkanes?	
17.10	How does boiling point change with the length of an alkane?	
17.11	How does viscosity change with the length of an alkane?	
17.12	How does flammability change with the length of an alkane?	
17.13	What is fractional distillation?	
17.14	What are the steps involved in fractional distillation?	

Section 18: Organic Chemistry 2

ANSWER KEY

18.1	Why is fractional distillation important?	Because the different fractions have different uses
18.2	What is a fuel?	A substance which when reacted with oxygen releases energy
18.3	Name five fuels we obtain from crude oil	Petrol, diesel, kerosene, heavy fuel oil and liquefied petroleum gases
18.4	What other uses are there for products of fractional distillation?	Solvents, lubricants, polymers and detergents
18.5	What is combustion?	The reaction of a fuel with oxygen
18.6	What are the products of complete combustion?	Carbon dioxide and water
18.7	When does incomplete combustion occur?	When there is not enough oxygen present
18.8	What is cracking?	The process of breaking down a long hydrocarbon into smaller hydrocarbons
18.9	What are the products of cracking?	Short alkanes and alkenes
18.10	Why is cracking important?	Because smaller hydrocarbons are more useful than longer ones
18.11	What are the two types of cracking?	Catalytic and steam cracking
18.12	What are alkenes	A different type of hydrocarbon which is more reactive than an alkane
18.13	What are alkenes used for?	As a starting material to make more useful chemicals
18.14	How do you test for an alkene?	React it with bromine water
18.15	What is the colour change when an alkene reacts with bromine water?	Turns from orange to colourless

TRACKER

Quiz	Date	Score
1		
2		
3		
4		
5		
6		

Got it? ☐

18.1	Why is fractional distillation important?	
18.2	What is a fuel?	
18.3	Name five fuels we obtain from crude oil	
18.4	What other uses are there for products of fractional distillation?	
18.5	What is combustion?	
18.6	What are the products of complete combustion?	
18.7	When does incomplete combustion occur?	
18.8	What is cracking?	
18.9	What are the products of cracking?	
18.10	Why is cracking important?	
18.11	What are the two types of cracking?	
18.12	What are alkenes	
18.13	What are alkenes used for?	
18.14	How do you test for an alkene?	
18.15	What is the colour change when an alkene reacts with bromine water?	

Section 18: Organic Chemistry 2

18.1	Why is fractional distillation important?	
18.2	What is a fuel?	
18.3	Name five fuels we obtain from crude oil	
18.4	What other uses are there for products of fractional distillation?	
18.5	What is combustion?	
18.6	What are the products of complete combustion?	
18.7	When does incomplete combustion occur?	
18.8	What is cracking?	
18.9	What are the products of cracking?	
18.10	Why is cracking important?	
18.11	What are the two types of cracking?	
18.12	What are alkenes	
18.13	What are alkenes used for?	
18.14	How do you test for an alkene?	
18.15	What is the colour change when an alkene reacts with bromine water?	

18.1	Why is fractional distillation important?	
18.2	What is a fuel?	
18.3	Name five fuels we obtain from crude oil	
18.4	What other uses are there for products of fractional distillation?	
18.5	What is combustion?	
18.6	What are the products of complete combustion?	
18.7	When does incomplete combustion occur?	
18.8	What is cracking?	
18.9	What are the products of cracking?	
18.10	Why is cracking important?	
18.11	What are the two types of cracking?	
18.12	What are alkenes	
18.13	What are alkenes used for?	
18.14	How do you test for an alkene?	
18.15	What is the colour change when an alkene reacts with bromine water?	

Section 18: Organic Chemistry 2

18.1	Why is fractional distillation important?	
18.2	What is a fuel?	
18.3	Name five fuels we obtain from crude oil	
18.4	What other uses are there for products of fractional distillation?	
18.5	What is combustion?	
18.6	What are the products of complete combustion?	
18.7	When does incomplete combustion occur?	
18.8	What is cracking?	
18.9	What are the products of cracking?	
18.10	Why is cracking important?	
18.11	What are the two types of cracking?	
18.12	What are alkenes	
18.13	What are alkenes used for?	
18.14	How do you test for an alkene?	
18.15	What is the colour change when an alkene reacts with bromine water?	

Section 18: Organic Chemistry 2

18.1	Why is fractional distillation important?	
18.2	What is a fuel?	
18.3	Name five fuels we obtain from crude oil	
18.4	What other uses are there for products of fractional distillation?	
18.5	What is combustion?	
18.6	What are the products of complete combustion?	
18.7	When does incomplete combustion occur?	
18.8	What is cracking?	
18.9	What are the products of cracking?	
18.10	Why is cracking important?	
18.11	What are the two types of cracking?	
18.12	What are alkenes	
18.13	What are alkenes used for?	
18.14	How do you test for an alkene?	
18.15	What is the colour change when an alkene reacts with bromine water?	

18.1	Why is fractional distillation important?	
18.2	What is a fuel?	
18.3	Name five fuels we obtain from crude oil	
18.4	What other uses are there for products of fractional distillation?	
18.5	What is combustion?	
18.6	What are the products of complete combustion?	
18.7	When does incomplete combustion occur?	
18.8	What is cracking?	
18.9	What are the products of cracking?	
18.10	Why is cracking important?	
18.11	What are the two types of cracking?	
18.12	What are alkenes	
18.13	What are alkenes used for?	
18.14	How do you test for an alkene?	
18.15	What is the colour change when an alkene reacts with bromine water?	

Section 19: Chemical Analysis 1

ANSWER KEY

19.1	What is chemical analysis?	The process of establishing what chemicals are present in a substance
19.2	In everyday language what is a "pure" substance?	A substance that has had nothing added to it and is in its "natural" state
19.3	In chemistry what is a "pure" substance?	A substance made of a single element or compound
19.4	How can pure substances be distinguished from impure ones?	By their melting/boiling points
19.5	Describe the melting and boiling points of pure substances	One very specific temperature
19.6	Describe the melting and boiling points of impure substances	They change state at a range of temperatures
19.7	What is a formulation?	A complex mixture designed as a useful product
19.8	Give three examples of formulations	fuels, cleaning agents, paints, medicines, alloys, fertilisers and foods
19.9	What is chromatography?	A process to separate the constituents of a mixture
19.10	In paper chromatography, what is the stationary phase and what is the mobile phase	Paper is stationary, solvent (usually water or ethanol) is mobile
19.11	How can chromatography show the difference between pure and impure substances?	Pure ones will not separate into a number of spots
19.12	How is the Rf value calculated?	distance moved by spot/ distance moved by solvent

TRACKER

Quiz	Date	Score
1		
2		
3		
4		
5		
6		

Got it? ☐

Section 19: Chemical Analysis 1

19.1	What is chemical analysis?	
19.2	In everyday language what is a "pure" substance?	
19.3	In chemistry what is a "pure" substance?	
19.4	How can pure substances be distinguished from impure ones?	
19.5	Describe the melting and boiling points of pure substances	
19.6	Describe the melting and boiling points of impure substances	
19.7	What is a formulation?	
19.8	Give three examples of formulations	
19.9	What is chromatography?	
19.10	In paper chromatography, what is the stationary phase and what is the mobile phase	
19.11	How can chromatography show the difference between pure and impure substances?	
19.12	How is the Rf value calculated?	

19.1	What is chemical analysis?	
19.2	In everyday language what is a "pure" substance?	
19.3	In chemistry what is a "pure" substance?	
19.4	How can pure substances be distinguished from impure ones?	
19.5	Describe the melting and boiling points of pure substances	
19.6	Describe the melting and boiling points of impure substances	
19.7	What is a formulation?	
19.8	Give three examples of formulations	
19.9	What is chromatography?	
19.10	In paper chromatography, what is the stationary phase and what is the mobile phase	
19.11	How can chromatography show the difference between pure and impure substances?	
19.12	How is the Rf value calculated?	

19.1	What is chemical analysis?	
19.2	In everyday language what is a "pure" substance?	
19.3	In chemistry what is a "pure" substance?	
19.4	How can pure substances be distinguished from impure ones?	
19.5	Describe the melting and boiling points of pure substances	
19.6	Describe the melting and boiling points of impure substances	
19.7	What is a formulation?	
19.8	Give three examples of formulations	
19.9	What is chromatography?	
19.10	In paper chromatography, what is the stationary phase and what is the mobile phase	
19.11	How can chromatography show the difference between pure and impure substances?	
19.12	How is the Rf value calculated?	

19.1	What is chemical analysis?	
19.2	In everyday language what is a "pure" substance?	
19.3	In chemistry what is a "pure" substance?	
19.4	How can pure substances be distinguished from impure ones?	
19.5	Describe the melting and boiling points of pure substances	
19.6	Describe the melting and boiling points of impure substances	
19.7	What is a formulation?	
19.8	Give three examples of formulations	
19.9	What is chromatography?	
19.10	In paper chromatography, what is the stationary phase and what is the mobile phase	
19.11	How can chromatography show the difference between pure and impure substances?	
19.12	How is the Rf value calculated?	

19.1	What is chemical analysis?	
19.2	In everyday language what is a "pure" substance?	
19.3	In chemistry what is a "pure" substance?	
19.4	How can pure substances be distinguished from impure ones?	
19.5	Describe the melting and boiling points of pure substances	
19.6	Describe the melting and boiling points of impure substances	
19.7	What is a formulation?	
19.8	Give three examples of formulations	
19.9	What is chromatography?	
19.10	In paper chromatography, what is the stationary phase and what is the mobile phase	
19.11	How can chromatography show the difference between pure and impure substances?	
19.12	How is the Rf value calculated?	

19.1	What is chemical analysis?	
19.2	In everyday language what is a "pure" substance?	
19.3	In chemistry what is a "pure" substance?	
19.4	How can pure substances be distinguished from impure ones?	
19.5	Describe the melting and boiling points of pure substances	
19.6	Describe the melting and boiling points of impure substances	
19.7	What is a formulation?	
19.8	Give three examples of formulations	
19.9	What is chromatography?	
19.10	In paper chromatography, what is the stationary phase and what is the mobile phase	
19.11	How can chromatography show the difference between pure and impure substances?	
19.12	How is the Rf value calculated?	

Section 20: Chemical Analysis 2

ANSWER KEY

20.1	What does a substance's Rf value depend on?	How soluble it is in the solvent
20.2	In chromatography, why must the substances be placed on a pencil line?	Pencil will not dissolve in the solvent
20.3	In chromatography why must the solvent height be lower than the pencil line?	So that the substances do not dissolve into the solvent off the paper
20.4	How can hydrogen be tested for?	Makes a squeaky pop when a splint is placed in it
20.5	How can oxygen be tested for?	Relights a glowing splint
20.6	How can carbon dioxide be tested for?	Bubble through limewater, turns it milky (cloudy)
20.7	How can chlorine be tested for?	Bleaches damp litmus paper white

TRACKER

Quiz	Date	Score
1		
2		
3		
4		
5		
6		

Got it? ☐

20.1	What does a substance's Rf value depend on?	
20.2	In chromatography, why must the substances be placed on a pencil line?	
20.3	In chromatography why must the solvent height be lower than the pencil line?	
20.4	How can hydrogen be tested for?	
20.5	How can oxygen be tested for?	
20.6	How can carbon dioxide be tested for?	
20.7	How can chlorine be tested for?	

Section 20: Chemical Analysis 2

20.1	What does a substance's Rf value depend on?	
20.2	In chromatography, why must the substances be placed on a pencil line?	
20.3	In chromatography why must the solvent height be lower than the pencil line?	
20.4	How can hydrogen be tested for?	
20.5	How can oxygen be tested for?	
20.6	How can carbon dioxide be tested for?	
20.7	How can chlorine be tested for?	

20.1	What does a substance's Rf value depend on?	
20.2	In chromatography, why must the substances be placed on a pencil line?	
20.3	In chromatography why must the solvent height be lower than the pencil line?	
20.4	How can hydrogen be tested for?	
20.5	How can oxygen be tested for?	
20.6	How can carbon dioxide be tested for?	
20.7	How can chlorine be tested for?	

20.1	What does a substance's Rf value depend on?	
20.2	In chromatography, why must the substances be placed on a pencil line?	
20.3	In chromatography why must the solvent height be lower than the pencil line?	
20.4	How can hydrogen be tested for?	
20.5	How can oxygen be tested for?	
20.6	How can carbon dioxide be tested for?	
20.7	How can chlorine be tested for?	

20.1	What does a substance's Rf value depend on?	
20.2	In chromatography, why must the substances be placed on a pencil line?	
20.3	In chromatography why must the solvent height be lower than the pencil line?	
20.4	How can hydrogen be tested for?	
20.5	How can oxygen be tested for?	
20.6	How can carbon dioxide be tested for?	
20.7	How can chlorine be tested for?	

20.1	What does a substance's Rf value depend on?	
20.2	In chromatography, why must the substances be placed on a pencil line?	
20.3	In chromatography why must the solvent height be lower than the pencil line?	
20.4	How can hydrogen be tested for?	
20.5	How can oxygen be tested for?	
20.6	How can carbon dioxide be tested for?	
20.7	How can chlorine be tested for?	

Section 21: Chemistry of the Atmosphere 1

ANSWER KEY

21.1	What is the approximate proportion of nitrogen in Earth's current atmosphere?	80%
21.2	What is the approximate proportion of oxygen in Earth's current atmosphere?	20%
21.3	Which gases are in small proportions in the current atmosphere?	Noble gases, water vapour, carbon dioxide
21.4	When Earth was formed which planets was its atmosphere similar to?	Venus and Mars
21.5	What do Mars and Venus's atmospheres comprise of?	Carbon dioxide with little or no oxygen
21.6	What produced the gases present in Earth's early atmosphere?	Volcanoes
21.7	Which gases were present in Earth's early atmosphere?	Carbon dioxide water vapour and nitrogen with small amounts of methane and ammonia
21.8	Why have theories about Earth's early atmosphere developed and changed over time?	Evidence is limited and it was billions of years ago
21.9	By what process do algae and plants produce oxygen?	Photosynthesis
21.10	Write the word equation to represent photosynthesis	carbon dioxide + water → oxygen + glucose
21.11	How did the world's oceans form?	The Earth's temperature cooled, causing water vapour in the air to condense
21.12	How did the oceans reduce atmospheric levels of carbon dioxide in Earth's early atmosphere?	Carbon dioxide dissolved in the oceans

TRACKER

Quiz	Date	Score
1		
2		
3		
4		
5		
6		

Got it? ☐

21.1	What is the approximate proportion of nitrogen in Earth's current atmosphere?	
21.2	What is the approximate proportion of oxygen in Earth's current atmosphere?	
21.3	Which gases are in small proportions in the current atmosphere?	
21.4	When Earth was formed which planets was its atmosphere similar to?	
21.5	What do Mars and Venus's atmospheres comprise of?	
21.6	What produced the gases present in Earth's early atmosphere?	
21.7	Which gases were present in Earth's early atmosphere?	
21.8	Why have theories about Earth's early atmosphere developed and changed over time?	
21.9	By what process do algae and plants produce oxygen?	
21.10	Write the word equation to represent photosynthesis	
21.11	How did the world's oceans form?	
21.12	How did the oceans reduce atmospheric levels of carbon dioxide in Earth's early atmosphere?	

Section 21: Chemistry of the Atmosphere 1

21.1	What is the approximate proportion of nitrogen in Earth's current atmosphere?	
21.2	What is the approximate proportion of oxygen in Earth's current atmosphere?	
21.3	Which gases are in small proportions in the current atmosphere?	
21.4	When Earth was formed which planets was its atmosphere similar to?	
21.5	What do Mars and Venus's atmospheres comprise of?	
21.6	What produced the gases present in Earth's early atmosphere?	
21.7	Which gases were present in Earth's early atmosphere?	
21.8	Why have theories about Earth's early atmosphere developed and changed over time?	
21.9	By what process do algae and plants produce oxygen?	
21.10	Write the word equation to represent photosynthesis	
21.11	How did the world's oceans form?	
21.12	How did the oceans reduce atmospheric levels of carbon dioxide in Earth's early atmosphere?	

21.1	What is the approximate proportion of nitrogen in Earth's current atmosphere?	
21.2	What is the approximate proportion of oxygen in Earth's current atmosphere?	
21.3	Which gases are in small proportions in the current atmosphere?	
21.4	When Earth was formed which planets was its atmosphere similar to?	
21.5	What do Mars and Venus's atmospheres comprise of?	
21.6	What produced the gases present in Earth's early atmosphere?	
21.7	Which gases were present in Earth's early atmosphere?	
21.8	Why have theories about Earth's early atmosphere developed and changed over time?	
21.9	By what process do algae and plants produce oxygen?	
21.10	Write the word equation to represent photosynthesis	
21.11	How did the world's oceans form?	
21.12	How did the oceans reduce atmospheric levels of carbon dioxide in Earth's early atmosphere?	

21.1	What is the approximate proportion of nitrogen in Earth's current atmosphere?	
21.2	What is the approximate proportion of oxygen in Earth's current atmosphere?	
21.3	Which gases are in small proportions in the current atmosphere?	
21.4	When Earth was formed which planets was its atmosphere similar to?	
21.5	What do Mars and Venus's atmospheres comprise of?	
21.6	What produced the gases present in Earth's early atmosphere?	
21.7	Which gases were present in Earth's early atmosphere?	
21.8	Why have theories about Earth's early atmosphere developed and changed over time?	
21.9	By what process do algae and plants produce oxygen?	
21.10	Write the word equation to represent photosynthesis	
21.11	How did the world's oceans form?	
21.12	How did the oceans reduce atmospheric levels of carbon dioxide in Earth's early atmosphere?	

21.1	What is the approximate proportion of nitrogen in Earth's current atmosphere?	
21.2	What is the approximate proportion of oxygen in Earth's current atmosphere?	
21.3	Which gases are in small proportions in the current atmosphere?	
21.4	When Earth was formed which planets was its atmosphere similar to?	
21.5	What do Mars and Venus's atmospheres comprise of?	
21.6	What produced the gases present in Earth's early atmosphere?	
21.7	Which gases were present in Earth's early atmosphere?	
21.8	Why have theories about Earth's early atmosphere developed and changed over time?	
21.9	By what process do algae and plants produce oxygen?	
21.10	Write the word equation to represent photosynthesis	
21.11	How did the world's oceans form?	
21.12	How did the oceans reduce atmospheric levels of carbon dioxide in Earth's early atmosphere?	

21.1	What is the approximate proportion of nitrogen in Earth's current atmosphere?	
21.2	What is the approximate proportion of oxygen in Earth's current atmosphere?	
21.3	Which gases are in small proportions in the current atmosphere?	
21.4	When Earth was formed which planets was its atmosphere similar to?	
21.5	What do Mars and Venus's atmospheres comprise of?	
21.6	What produced the gases present in Earth's early atmosphere?	
21.7	Which gases were present in Earth's early atmosphere?	
21.8	Why have theories about Earth's early atmosphere developed and changed over time?	
21.9	By what process do algae and plants produce oxygen?	
21.10	Write the word equation to represent photosynthesis	
21.11	How did the world's oceans form?	
21.12	How did the oceans reduce atmospheric levels of carbon dioxide in Earth's early atmosphere?	

ANSWER KEY

22.1	How did algae and plants reduce levels of carbon dioxide in Earth's early atmosphere?	By photosynthesising
22.2	What was formed when shells of organisms made using dissolved carbon dioxide, fell to the bottom of the ocean and were covered and compressed?	Sedimentary rock
22.3	What was formed when plants that grew millions of years ago, died and were trapped and compressed under rocks?	Coal
22.4	What was formed when plankton that lived in the ocean millions of years ago, died and were trapped and compressed under rocks?	Crude Oil and Natural Gas
22.5	Name three greenhouse gases	Water Vapour, Carbon Dioxide and Methane
22.6	Describe the wavelength of radiation that comes from the sun and is reflected by the Earth	From the Sun: short wave, From the Earth: long wave
22.7	What happens to the long wave radiation that is reflected from the Earth in the atmosphere?	It is absorbed by the greenhouse gases
22.8	What is the name given to the process that warms of the surface of the Earth?	The greenhouse effect
22.9	What human activities increase carbon dioxide levels?	Deforestation and burning fossil fuels
22.10	What human activities increase methane levels?	Farming animals and landfill
22.11	What is the name given to the increasing average temperature of the Earth?	Climate Change
22.12	Name an effect of climate change	Increased flooding, changes in rainfall patterns, frequency of storms, amount of water in a habitat etc...

TRACKER

Quiz	Date	Score
1		
2		
3		
4		
5		
6		

Got it? ☐

Section 22: Chemistry of the Atmosphere 2

22.1	How did algae and plants reduce levels of carbon dioxide in Earth's early atmosphere?	
22.2	What was formed when shells of organisms made using dissolved carbon dioxide, fell to the bottom of the ocean and were covered and compressed?	
22.3	What was formed when plants that grew millions of years ago, died and were trapped and compressed under rocks?	
22.4	What was formed when plankton that lived in the ocean millions of years ago, died and were trapped and compressed under rocks?	
22.5	Name three greenhouse gases	
22.6	Describe the wavelength of radiation that comes from the sun and is reflected by the Earth	
22.7	What happens to the long wave radiation that is reflected from the Earth in the atmosphere?	
22.8	What is the name given to the process that warms of the surface of the Earth?	
22.9	What human activities increase carbon dioxide levels?	
22.10	What human activities increase methane levels?	
22.11	What is the name given to the increasing average temperature of the Earth?	
22.12	Name an effect of climate change	

22.1	How did algae and plants reduce levels of carbon dioxide in Earth's early atmosphere?	
22.2	What was formed when shells of organisms made using dissolved carbon dioxide, fell to the bottom of the ocean and were covered and compressed?	
22.3	What was formed when plants that grew millions of years ago, died and were trapped and compressed under rocks?	
22.4	What was formed when plankton that lived in the ocean millions of years ago, died and were trapped and compressed under rocks?	
22.5	Name three greenhouse gases	
22.6	Describe the wavelength of radiation that comes from the sun and is reflected by the Earth	
22.7	What happens to the long wave radiation that is reflected from the Earth in the atmosphere?	
22.8	What is the name given to the process that warms of the surface of the Earth?	
22.9	What human activities increase carbon dioxide levels?	
22.10	What human activities increase methane levels?	
22.11	What is the name given to the increasing average temperature of the Earth?	
22.12	Name an effect of climate change	

Section 22: Chemistry of the Atmosphere 2

22.1	How did algae and plants reduce levels of carbon dioxide in Earth's early atmosphere?	
22.2	What was formed when shells of organisms made using dissolved carbon dioxide, fell to the bottom of the ocean and were covered and compressed?	
22.3	What was formed when plants that grew millions of years ago, died and were trapped and compressed under rocks?	
22.4	What was formed when plankton that lived in the ocean millions of years ago, died and were trapped and compressed under rocks?	
22.5	Name three greenhouse gases	
22.6	Describe the wavelength of radiation that comes from the sun and is reflected by the Earth	
22.7	What happens to the long wave radiation that is reflected from the Earth in the atmosphere?	
22.8	What is the name given to the process that warms of the surface of the Earth?	
22.9	What human activities increase carbon dioxide levels?	
22.10	What human activities increase methane levels?	
22.11	What is the name given to the increasing average temperature of the Earth?	
22.12	Name an effect of climate change	

22.1	How did algae and plants reduce levels of carbon dioxide in Earth's early atmosphere?	
22.2	What was formed when shells of organisms made using dissolved carbon dioxide, fell to the bottom of the ocean and were covered and compressed?	
22.3	What was formed when plants that grew millions of years ago, died and were trapped and compressed under rocks?	
22.4	What was formed when plankton that lived in the ocean millions of years ago, died and were trapped and compressed under rocks?	
22.5	Name three greenhouse gases	
22.6	Describe the wavelength of radiation that comes from the sun and is reflected by the Earth	
22.7	What happens to the long wave radiation that is reflected from the Earth in the atmosphere?	
22.8	What is the name given to the process that warms of the surface of the Earth?	
22.9	What human activities increase carbon dioxide levels?	
22.10	What human activities increase methane levels?	
22.11	What is the name given to the increasing average temperature of the Earth?	
22.12	Name an effect of climate change	

22.1	How did algae and plants reduce levels of carbon dioxide in Earth's early atmosphere?	
22.2	What was formed when shells of organisms made using dissolved carbon dioxide, fell to the bottom of the ocean and were covered and compressed?	
22.3	What was formed when plants that grew millions of years ago, died and were trapped and compressed under rocks?	
22.4	What was formed when plankton that lived in the ocean millions of years ago, died and were trapped and compressed under rocks?	
22.5	Name three greenhouse gases	
22.6	Describe the wavelength of radiation that comes from the sun and is reflected by the Earth	
22.7	What happens to the long wave radiation that is reflected from the Earth in the atmosphere?	
22.8	What is the name given to the process that warms of the surface of the Earth?	
22.9	What human activities increase carbon dioxide levels?	
22.10	What human activities increase methane levels?	
22.11	What is the name given to the increasing average temperature of the Earth?	
22.12	Name an effect of climate change	

22.1	How did algae and plants reduce levels of carbon dioxide in Earth's early atmosphere?	
22.2	What was formed when shells of organisms made using dissolved carbon dioxide, fell to the bottom of the ocean and were covered and compressed?	
22.3	What was formed when plants that grew millions of years ago, died and were trapped and compressed under rocks?	
22.4	What was formed when plankton that lived in the ocean millions of years ago, died and were trapped and compressed under rocks?	
22.5	Name three greenhouse gases	
22.6	Describe the wavelength of radiation that comes from the sun and is reflected by the Earth	
22.7	What happens to the long wave radiation that is reflected from the Earth in the atmosphere?	
22.8	What is the name given to the process that warms of the surface of the Earth?	
22.9	What human activities increase carbon dioxide levels?	
22.10	What human activities increase methane levels?	
22.11	What is the name given to the increasing average temperature of the Earth?	
22.12	Name an effect of climate change	

ANSWER KEY

23.1	What is the name given to the total amount of carbon dioxide and other greenhouse gases emitted over the full lifecycle of a product, service or event?	Carbon footprint
23.2	What is produced from the complete combustion of a hydrocarbon fuel?	carbon dioxide and water
23.3	Which products could be produced from the incomplete combustion of a hydrocarbon fuel?	carbon dioxide, water, carbon monoxide, carbon particulates
23.4	Which gas is produced when fuels are burned and contain sulfur impurities?	sulfur dioxide
23.5	Which gases are produced when nitrogen and oxygen react in the very high temperatures of a car engine?	oxides of nitrogen
23.6	What are the effects of carbon monoxide?	a toxic gas
23.7	What are the effects of sulfur dioxide?	causes respiratory problems and acid rain
23.8	What are the effects of the oxides of nitrogen?	causes respiratory problems and acid rain
23.9	What are the effects of particulates of fuels?	cause global dimming and health problems for humans

TRACKER

Quiz	Date	Score
1		
2		
3		
4		
5		
6		

Got it? ☐

23.1	What is the name given to the total amount of carbon dioxide and other greenhouse gases emitted over the full lifecycle of a product, service or event?	
23.2	What is produced from the complete combustion of a hydrocarbon fuel?	
23.3	Which products could be produced from the incomplete combustion of a hydrocarbon fuel?	
23.4	Which gas is produced when fuels are burned and contain sulfur impurities?	
23.5	Which gases are produced when nitrogen and oxygen react in the very high temperatures of a car engine?	
23.6	What are the effects of carbon monoxide?	
23.7	What are the effects of sulfur dioxide?	
23.8	What are the effects of the oxides of nitrogen?	
23.9	What are the effects of particulates of fuels?	

23.1	What is the name given to the total amount of carbon dioxide and other greenhouse gases emitted over the full lifecycle of a product, service or event?	
23.2	What is produced from the complete combustion of a hydrocarbon fuel?	
23.3	Which products could be produced from the incomplete combustion of a hydrocarbon fuel?	
23.4	Which gas is produced when fuels are burned and contain sulfur impurities?	
23.5	Which gases are produced when nitrogen and oxygen react in the very high temperatures of a car engine?	
23.6	What are the effects of carbon monoxide?	
23.7	What are the effects of sulfur dioxide?	
23.8	What are the effects of the oxides of nitrogen?	
23.9	What are the effects of particulates of fuels?	

23.1	What is the name given to the total amount of carbon dioxide and other greenhouse gases emitted over the full lifecycle of a product, service or event?	
23.2	What is produced from the complete combustion of a hydrocarbon fuel?	
23.3	Which products could be produced from the incomplete combustion of a hydrocarbon fuel?	
23.4	Which gas is produced when fuels are burned and contain sulfur impurities?	
23.5	Which gases are produced when nitrogen and oxygen react in the very high temperatures of a car engine?	
23.6	What are the effects of carbon monoxide?	
23.7	What are the effects of sulfur dioxide?	
23.8	What are the effects of the oxides of nitrogen?	
23.9	What are the effects of particulates of fuels?	

23.1	What is the name given to the total amount of carbon dioxide and other greenhouse gases emitted over the full lifecycle of a product, service or event?	
23.2	What is produced from the complete combustion of a hydrocarbon fuel?	
23.3	Which products could be produced from the incomplete combustion of a hydrocarbon fuel?	
23.4	Which gas is produced when fuels are burned and contain sulfur impurities?	
23.5	Which gases are produced when nitrogen and oxygen react in the very high temperatures of a car engine?	
23.6	What are the effects of carbon monoxide?	
23.7	What are the effects of sulfur dioxide?	
23.8	What are the effects of the oxides of nitrogen?	
23.9	What are the effects of particulates of fuels?	

23.1	What is the name given to the total amount of carbon dioxide and other greenhouse gases emitted over the full lifecycle of a product, service or event?	
23.2	What is produced from the complete combustion of a hydrocarbon fuel?	
23.3	Which products could be produced from the incomplete combustion of a hydrocarbon fuel?	
23.4	Which gas is produced when fuels are burned and contain sulfur impurities?	
23.5	Which gases are produced when nitrogen and oxygen react in the very high temperatures of a car engine?	
23.6	What are the effects of carbon monoxide?	
23.7	What are the effects of sulfur dioxide?	
23.8	What are the effects of the oxides of nitrogen?	
23.9	What are the effects of particulates of fuels?	

23.1	What is the name given to the total amount of carbon dioxide and other greenhouse gases emitted over the full lifecycle of a product, service or event?	
23.2	What is produced from the complete combustion of a hydrocarbon fuel?	
23.3	Which products could be produced from the incomplete combustion of a hydrocarbon fuel?	
23.4	Which gas is produced when fuels are burned and contain sulfur impurities?	
23.5	Which gases are produced when nitrogen and oxygen react in the very high temperatures of a car engine?	
23.6	What are the effects of carbon monoxide?	
23.7	What are the effects of sulfur dioxide?	
23.8	What are the effects of the oxides of nitrogen?	
23.9	What are the effects of particulates of fuels?	

ANSWER KEY

24.1	What do humans use resources for?	Warmth, shelter and food
24.2	What are finite resources?	Resources that will run out
24.3	What is sustainable development?	Development that meets the needs of the current generations without compromising the ability of future generations to meet their own needs
24.4	Give an example of a natural product that has been replaced by a synthetic product	Cotton has been replaced by polyester
24.5	What is potable water?	Water that is safe to drink
24.6	In the UK how is potable water produced?	Passing fresh water through filter beds and sterilising
24.7	How is water sterilised?	Using chlorine, ozone or ultraviolet light
24.8	What is desalination?	Removal of saly from sea water
24.9	In what two ways can desalination be carried out?	Reverse osmosis or distillation
24.10	What is the main disadvantage of desalination?	It requires a large amount of energy
24.11	In what kinds of locations is desalination carried out?	Ones where there is limited supply of fresh water
24.12	What needs to be removed from sewage and agricultural waste water?	Organic matter and harmful microbes

TRACKER

Quiz	Date	Score
1		
2		
3		
4		
5		
6		

Got it? ☐

24.1	What do humans use resources for?	
24.2	What are finite resources?	
24.3	What is sustainable development?	
24.4	Give an example of a natural product that has been replaced by a synthetic product	
24.5	What is potable water?	
24.6	In the UK how is potable water produced?	
24.7	How is water sterilised?	
24.8	What is desalination?	
24.9	In what two ways can desalination be carried out?	
24.10	What is the main disadvantage of desalination?	
24.11	In what kinds of locations is desalination carried out?	
24.12	What needs to be removed from sewage and agricultural waste water?	

24.1	What do humans use resources for?	
24.2	What are finite resources?	
24.3	What is sustainable development?	
24.4	Give an example of a natural product that has been replaced by a synthetic product	
24.5	What is potable water?	
24.6	In the UK how is potable water produced?	
24.7	How is water sterilised?	
24.8	What is desalination?	
24.9	In what two ways can desalination be carried out?	
24.10	What is the main disadvantage of desalination?	
24.11	In what kinds of locations is desalination carried out?	
24.12	What needs to be removed from sewage and agricultural waste water?	

24.1	What do humans use resources for?	
24.2	What are finite resources?	
24.3	What is sustainable development?	
24.4	Give an example of a natural product that has been replaced by a synthetic product	
24.5	What is potable water?	
24.6	In the UK how is potable water produced?	
24.7	How is water sterilised?	
24.8	What is desalination?	
24.9	In what two ways can desalination be carried out?	
24.10	What is the main disadvantage of desalination?	
24.11	In what kinds of locations is desalination carried out?	
24.12	What needs to be removed from sewage and agricultural waste water?	

24.1	What do humans use resources for?	
24.2	What are finite resources?	
24.3	What is sustainable development?	
24.4	Give an example of a natural product that has been replaced by a synthetic product	
24.5	What is potable water?	
24.6	In the UK how is potable water produced?	
24.7	How is water sterilised?	
24.8	What is desalination?	
24.9	In what two ways can desalination be carried out?	
24.10	What is the main disadvantage of desalination?	
24.11	In what kinds of locations is desalination carried out?	
24.12	What needs to be removed from sewage and agricultural waste water?	

24.1	What do humans use resources for?	
24.2	What are finite resources?	
24.3	What is sustainable development?	
24.4	Give an example of a natural product that has been replaced by a synthetic product	
24.5	What is potable water?	
24.6	In the UK how is potable water produced?	
24.7	How is water sterilised?	
24.8	What is desalination?	
24.9	In what two ways can desalination be carried out?	
24.10	What is the main disadvantage of desalination?	
24.11	In what kinds of locations is desalination carried out?	
24.12	What needs to be removed from sewage and agricultural waste water?	

24.1	What do humans use resources for?	
24.2	What are finite resources?	
24.3	What is sustainable development?	
24.4	Give an example of a natural product that has been replaced by a synthetic product	
24.5	What is potable water?	
24.6	In the UK how is potable water produced?	
24.7	How is water sterilised?	
24.8	What is desalination?	
24.9	In what two ways can desalination be carried out?	
24.10	What is the main disadvantage of desalination?	
24.11	In what kinds of locations is desalination carried out?	
24.12	What needs to be removed from sewage and agricultural waste water?	

ANSWER KEY

25.1	What needs to be removed from industrial waste water?	Organic matter and harmful chemicals
25.2	How is sewage treated?	Screening, sedimentation, anaerobic digestion, aerobic biological treatment
25.3	(HT) Name two new ways of extracting copper from low-grade ores	Phytomining and bioleaching
25.4	(HT) What is a low grade ore?	Rock with only a small amount of metal compound in it
25.5	(HT) How is phytomining carried out?	Plants absorb metal compounds, are harvested and then burned to produce ash
25.6	(HT) How is bioleaching carried out?	Bacteria are used to produce a leachate solution
25.7	(HT) How can copper be produced from the products of phytomining or bioleaching?	Electrolysis or displacement with scrap iron
25.8	What is a life cycle assessment?	A way of assessing the environmental impact of a product across its entire life cycle
25.9	What are the four stages in a product's life cycle?	Extracting and processing raw materials, manufacturing and packaging, use and operation, disposal distribution at each stage.
25.10	Why is it important to reduce use, recycle and reuse products?	Reduces the use of limited resources, energy sources and environmental impacts
25.11	Give an example of a product that can be reused	Glass
25.12	Give an example of a product that can be recycled	Metal

TRACKER

Quiz	Date	Score
1		
2		
3		
4		
5		
6		

Got it? ☐

25.1	What needs to be removed from industrial waste water?	
25.2	How is sewage treated?	
25.3	(HT) Name two new ways of extracting copper from low-grade ores	
25.4	(HT) What is a low grade ore?	
25.5	(HT) How is phytomining carried out?	
25.6	(HT) How is bioleaching carried out?	
25.7	(HT) How can copper be produced from the products of phytomining or bioleaching?	
25.8	What is a life cycle assessment?	
25.9	What are the four stages in a product's life cycle?	
25.10	Why is it important to reduce use, recycle and reuse products?	
25.11	Give an example of a product that can be reused	
25.12	Give an example of a product that can be recycled	

25.1	What needs to be removed from industrial waste water?	
25.2	How is sewage treated?	
25.3	(HT) Name two new ways of extracting copper from low-grade ores	
25.4	(HT) What is a low grade ore?	
25.5	(HT) How is phytomining carried out?	
25.6	(HT) How is bioleaching carried out?	
25.7	(HT) How can copper be produced from the products of phytomining or bioleaching?	
25.8	What is a life cycle assessment?	
25.9	What are the four stages in a product's life cycle?	
25.10	Why is it important to reduce use, recycle and reuse products?	
25.11	Give an example of a product that can be reused	
25.12	Give an example of a product that can be recycled	

25.1	What needs to be removed from industrial waste water?	
25.2	How is sewage treated?	
25.3	(HT) Name two new ways of extracting copper from low-grade ores	
25.4	(HT) What is a low grade ore?	
25.5	(HT) How is phytomining carried out?	
25.6	(HT) How is bioleaching carried out?	
25.7	(HT) How can copper be produced from the products of phytomining or bioleaching?	
25.8	What is a life cycle assessment?	
25.9	What are the four stages in a product's life cycle?	
25.10	Why is it important to reduce use, recycle and reuse products?	
25.11	Give an example of a product that can be reused	
25.12	Give an example of a product that can be recycled	

25.1	What needs to be removed from industrial waste water?	
25.2	How is sewage treated?	
25.3	(HT) Name two new ways of extracting copper from low-grade ores	
25.4	(HT) What is a low grade ore?	
25.5	(HT) How is phytomining carried out?	
25.6	(HT) How is bioleaching carried out?	
25.7	(HT) How can copper be produced from the products of phytomining or bioleaching?	
25.8	What is a life cycle assessment?	
25.9	What are the four stages in a product's life cycle?	
25.10	Why is it important to reduce use, recycle and reuse products?	
25.11	Give an example of a product that can be reused	
25.12	Give an example of a product that can be recycled	

25.1	What needs to be removed from industrial waste water?	
25.2	How is sewage treated?	
25.3	(HT) Name two new ways of extracting copper from low-grade ores	
25.4	(HT) What is a low grade ore?	
25.5	(HT) How is phytomining carried out?	
25.6	(HT) How is bioleaching carried out?	
25.7	(HT) How can copper be produced from the products of phytomining or bioleaching?	
25.8	What is a life cycle assessment?	
25.9	What are the four stages in a product's life cycle?	
25.10	Why is it important to reduce use, recycle and reuse products?	
25.11	Give an example of a product that can be reused	
25.12	Give an example of a product that can be recycled	

25.1	What needs to be removed from industrial waste water?	
25.2	How is sewage treated?	
25.3	(HT) Name two new ways of extracting copper from low-grade ores	
25.4	(HT) What is a low grade ore?	
25.5	(HT) How is phytomining carried out?	
25.6	(HT) How is bioleaching carried out?	
25.7	(HT) How can copper be produced from the products of phytomining or bioleaching?	
25.8	What is a life cycle assessment?	
25.9	What are the four stages in a product's life cycle?	
25.10	Why is it important to reduce use, recycle and reuse products?	
25.11	Give an example of a product that can be reused	
25.12	Give an example of a product that can be recycled	

ANSWER KEY

26.1	Where are transition metals found in the periodic table?	In the middle
26.2	Compare the melting point, density, strength, hardness and reactivity of transition metals with group 1 metals	Higher for all but reactivity
26.3	What is distinctive about the ions formed by transition metals?	Can form ions with different charges
26.4	What is distinctive about compounds formed from transition metals?	They are coloured
26.5	What can transition metals be used for?	Catalysts
26.6	How big are nanoparticles?	1-100nm, a few hundred atoms
26.7	Calculate the surface area to volume ratio for a cube with side length 1cm.	6:1
26.8	Why do nanoparticles have different properties to bulk materials?	Because of their high SA:V ratio
26.9	Give two examples of what nanoparticles can be used for	Medical applications, sun creams, catalysts, deodorants, cosmetics, electronics

TRACKER

Quiz	Date	Score
1		
2		
3		
4		
5		
6		

Got it? ☐

26.1	Where are transition metals found in the periodic table?	
26.2	Compare the melting point, density, strength, hardness and reactivity of transition metals with group 1 metals	
26.3	What is distinctive about the ions formed by transition metals?	
26.4	What is distinctive about compounds formed from transition metals?	
26.5	What can transition metals be used for?	
26.6	How big are nanoparticles?	
26.7	Calculate the surface area to volume ratio for a cube with side length 1cm.	
26.8	Why do nanoparticles have different properties to bulk materials?	
26.9	Give two examples of what nanoparticles can be used for	

26.1	Where are transition metals found in the periodic table?	
26.2	Compare the melting point, density, strength, hardness and reactivity of transition metals with group 1 metals	
26.3	What is distinctive about the ions formed by transition metals?	
26.4	What is distinctive about compounds formed from transition metals?	
26.5	What can transition metals be used for?	
26.6	How big are nanoparticles?	
26.7	Calculate the surface area to volume ratio for a cube with side length 1cm.	
26.8	Why do nanoparticles have different properties to bulk materials?	
26.9	Give two examples of what nanoparticles can be used for	

26.1	Where are transition metals found in the periodic table?	
26.2	Compare the melting point, density, strength, hardness and reactivity of transition metals with group 1 metals	
26.3	What is distinctive about the ions formed by transition metals?	
26.4	What is distinctive about compounds formed from transition metals?	
26.5	What can transition metals be used for?	
26.6	How big are nanoparticles?	
26.7	Calculate the surface area to volume ratio for a cube with side length 1cm.	
26.8	Why do nanoparticles have different properties to bulk materials?	
26.9	Give two examples of what nanoparticles can be used for	

26.1	Where are transition metals found in the periodic table?	
26.2	Compare the melting point, density, strength, hardness and reactivity of transition metals with group 1 metals	
26.3	What is distinctive about the ions formed by transition metals?	
26.4	What is distinctive about compounds formed from transition metals?	
26.5	What can transition metals be used for?	
26.6	How big are nanoparticles?	
26.7	Calculate the surface area to volume ratio for a cube with side length 1cm.	
26.8	Why do nanoparticles have different properties to bulk materials?	
26.9	Give two examples of what nanoparticles can be used for	

26.1	Where are transition metals found in the periodic table?	
26.2	Compare the melting point, density, strength, hardness and reactivity of transition metals with group 1 metals	
26.3	What is distinctive about the ions formed by transition metals?	
26.4	What is distinctive about compounds formed from transition metals?	
26.5	What can transition metals be used for?	
26.6	How big are nanoparticles?	
26.7	Calculate the surface area to volume ratio for a cube with side length 1cm.	
26.8	Why do nanoparticles have different properties to bulk materials?	
26.9	Give two examples of what nanoparticles can be used for	

26.1	Where are transition metals found in the periodic table?	
26.2	Compare the melting point, density, strength, hardness and reactivity of transition metals with group 1 metals	
26.3	What is distinctive about the ions formed by transition metals?	
26.4	What is distinctive about compounds formed from transition metals?	
26.5	What can transition metals be used for?	
26.6	How big are nanoparticles?	
26.7	Calculate the surface area to volume ratio for a cube with side length 1cm.	
26.8	Why do nanoparticles have different properties to bulk materials?	
26.9	Give two examples of what nanoparticles can be used for	

Section 27: Further Quantitative (*Triple Content*)

ANSWER KEY

27.1	What is the yield of a chemical reaction?	The amount of useful product
27.2	What is the theoretical yield of a chemical reaction?	The yield which you would expect to get in a reaction
27.3	What is the percentage yield of a chemical reaction?	The mount of actual product divided by the theoretical yield
27.4	Why is the % yield almost never 100%?	Reversible reaction, loss of product on separation, unexpected side reactions
27.5	What is atom economy?	The amount of starting material that ends up as useful product
27.6	Why is atom economy important?	Economic and sustainability reasons
27.7	How is atom economy calculated?	100 x Mr desired product/ Mr of all reactants
27.8	(HT) What are the two units for concentration?	g/dm^3 and mol/dm^3
27.9	(HT) Which formula relates concentration, moles and volume?	concentration = moles/volume
27.10	What is the purpose of titration?	Establish the concentration of an unknown solution
27.11	(HT) What do the moles of gases and their volumes have in common?	At the same temperature they occupy the same amount of volume
27.12	(HT) What is the volume of one mole of any gas at room temperature and pressure?	$24dm^3$

TRACKER

Quiz	Date	Score
1		
2		
3		
4		
5		
6		

Got it? ☐

27.1	What is the yield of a chemical reaction?	
27.2	What is the theoretical yield of a chemical reaction?	
27.3	What is the percentage yield of a chemical reaction?	
27.4	Why is the % yield almost never 100%?	
27.5	What is atom economy?	
27.6	Why is atom economy important?	
27.7	How is atom economy calculated?	
27.8	(HT) What are the two units for concentration?	
27.9	(HT) Which formula relates concentration, moles and volume?	
27.10	What is the purpose of titration?	
27.11	(HT) What do the moles of gases and their volumes have in common?	
27.12	(HT) What is the volume of one mole of any gas at room temperature and pressure?	

27.1	What is the yield of a chemical reaction?	
27.2	What is the theoretical yield of a chemical reaction?	
27.3	What is the percentage yield of a chemical reaction?	
27.4	Why is the % yield almost never 100%?	
27.5	What is atom economy?	
27.6	Why is atom economy important?	
27.7	How is atom economy calculated?	
27.8	(HT) What are the two units for concentration?	
27.9	(HT) Which formula relates concentration, moles and volume?	
27.10	What is the purpose of titration?	
27.11	(HT) What do the moles of gases and their volumes have in common?	
27.12	(HT) What is the volume of one mole of any gas at room temperature and pressure?	

27.1	What is the yield of a chemical reaction?	
27.2	What is the theoretical yield of a chemical reaction?	
27.3	What is the percentage yield of a chemical reaction?	
27.4	Why is the % yield almost never 100%?	
27.5	What is atom economy?	
27.6	Why is atom economy important?	
27.7	How is atom economy calculated?	
27.8	(HT) What are the two units for concentration?	
27.9	(HT) Which formula relates concentration, moles and volume?	
27.10	What is the purpose of titration?	
27.11	(HT) What do the moles of gases and their volumes have in common?	
27.12	(HT) What is the volume of one mole of any gas at room temperature and pressure?	

27.1	What is the yield of a chemical reaction?	
27.2	What is the theoretical yield of a chemical reaction?	
27.3	What is the percentage yield of a chemical reaction?	
27.4	Why is the % yield almost never 100%?	
27.5	What is atom economy?	
27.6	Why is atom economy important?	
27.7	How is atom economy calculated?	
27.8	(HT) What are the two units for concentration?	
27.9	(HT) Which formula relates concentration, moles and volume?	
27.10	What is the purpose of titration?	
27.11	(HT) What do the moles of gases and their volumes have in common?	
27.12	(HT) What is the volume of one mole of any gas at room temperature and pressure?	

27.1	What is the yield of a chemical reaction?	
27.2	What is the theoretical yield of a chemical reaction?	
27.3	What is the percentage yield of a chemical reaction?	
27.4	Why is the % yield almost never 100%?	
27.5	What is atom economy?	
27.6	Why is atom economy important?	
27.7	How is atom economy calculated?	
27.8	(HT) What are the two units for concentration?	
27.9	(HT) Which formula relates concentration, moles and volume?	
27.10	What is the purpose of titration?	
27.11	(HT) What do the moles of gases and their volumes have in common?	
27.12	(HT) What is the volume of one mole of any gas at room temperature and pressure?	

27.1	What is the yield of a chemical reaction?	
27.2	What is the theoretical yield of a chemical reaction?	
27.3	What is the percentage yield of a chemical reaction?	
27.4	Why is the % yield almost never 100%?	
27.5	What is atom economy?	
27.6	Why is atom economy important?	
27.7	How is atom economy calculated?	
27.8	(HT) What are the two units for concentration?	
27.9	(HT) Which formula relates concentration, moles and volume?	
27.10	What is the purpose of titration?	
27.11	(HT) What do the moles of gases and their volumes have in common?	
27.12	(HT) What is the volume of one mole of any gas at room temperature and pressure?	

Section 28: Chemical and Fuel Cells (*Triple Content*)

ANSWER KEY

28.1	What is a chemical cell?	A unit which contains chemicals which produce electricity through a reaction
28.2	What are the main components of a chemical cell?	An anode, a cathode and an electrolyte
28.3	What is a battery?	Two or more cells connected in series
28.4	What happens to the electrodes in a chemical cell?	The more reactive metal depletes and the less reactive one increases in mass.
28.5	Why can some cells not be recharged?	Because the reaction is not reversible
28.6	How can certain cells be recharged?	Applying an external electric current
28.7	How does the reactivity of the metal electrodes affect the size of the potential difference?	The greater the difference in reactivity, the greater the potential difference.
28.8	What is a fuel cell?	A cell which uses a fuel and oxygen (or air) to generate electricity.
28.9	What are the products in a hydrogen fuel cell?	Water
28.10	State three advantages of hydrogen fuel cells	Do not need to be recharged, no pollutants are produced, can be different sizes for different uses
28.11	State three disadvantages of hydrogen fuel cells	Hydrogen is highly flammable, hydrogen is sometimes produced through non-renewable means, hydrogen is difficult to store
28.12	Give the overall equation in a hydrogen fuel cell	$2H_2 + O_2 \rightarrow 2H_2O$

TRACKER

Quiz	Date	Score
1		
2		
3		
4		
5		
6		

Got it? ☐

28.1	What is a chemical cell?	
28.2	What are the main components of a chemical cell?	
28.3	What is a battery?	
28.4	What happens to the electrodes in a chemical cell?	
28.5	Why can some cells not be recharged?	
28.6	How can certain cells be recharged?	
28.7	How does the reactivity of the metal electrodes affect the size of the potential difference?	
28.8	What is a fuel cell?	
28.9	What are the products in a hydrogen fuel cell?	
28.10	State three advantages of hydrogen fuel cells	
28.11	State three disadvantages of hydrogen fuel cells	
28.12	Give the overall equation in a hydrogen fuel cell	

28.1	What is a chemical cell?	
28.2	What are the main components of a chemical cell?	
28.3	What is a battery?	
28.4	What happens to the electrodes in a chemical cell?	
28.5	Why can some cells not be recharged?	
28.6	How can certain cells be recharged?	
28.7	How does the reactivity of the metal electrodes affect the size of the potential difference?	
28.8	What is a fuel cell?	
28.9	What are the products in a hydrogen fuel cell?	
28.10	State three advantages of hydrogen fuel cells	
28.11	State three disadvantages of hydrogen fuel cells	
28.12	Give the overall equation in a hydrogen fuel cell	

28.1	What is a chemical cell?	
28.2	What are the main components of a chemical cell?	
28.3	What is a battery?	
28.4	What happens to the electrodes in a chemical cell?	
28.5	Why can some cells not be recharged?	
28.6	How can certain cells be recharged?	
28.7	How does the reactivity of the metal electrodes affect the size of the potential difference?	
28.8	What is a fuel cell?	
28.9	What are the products in a hydrogen fuel cell?	
28.10	State three advantages of hydrogen fuel cells	
28.11	State three disadvantages of hydrogen fuel cells	
28.12	Give the overall equation in a hydrogen fuel cell	

28.1	What is a chemical cell?	
28.2	What are the main components of a chemical cell?	
28.3	What is a battery?	
28.4	What happens to the electrodes in a chemical cell?	
28.5	Why can some cells not be recharged?	
28.6	How can certain cells be recharged?	
28.7	How does the reactivity of the metal electrodes affect the size of the potential difference?	
28.8	What is a fuel cell?	
28.9	What are the products in a hydrogen fuel cell?	
28.10	State three advantages of hydrogen fuel cells	
28.11	State three disadvantages of hydrogen fuel cells	
28.12	Give the overall equation in a hydrogen fuel cell	

Section 28: Chemical and Fuel Cells (*Triple Content*)

28.1	What is a chemical cell?	
28.2	What are the main components of a chemical cell?	
28.3	What is a battery?	
28.4	What happens to the electrodes in a chemical cell?	
28.5	Why can some cells not be recharged?	
28.6	How can certain cells be recharged?	
28.7	How does the reactivity of the metal electrodes affect the size of the potential difference?	
28.8	What is a fuel cell?	
28.9	What are the products in a hydrogen fuel cell?	
28.10	State three advantages of hydrogen fuel cells	
28.11	State three disadvantages of hydrogen fuel cells	
28.12	Give the overall equation in a hydrogen fuel cell	

28.1	What is a chemical cell?	
28.2	What are the main components of a chemical cell?	
28.3	What is a battery?	
28.4	What happens to the electrodes in a chemical cell?	
28.5	Why can some cells not be recharged?	
28.6	How can certain cells be recharged?	
28.7	How does the reactivity of the metal electrodes affect the size of the potential difference?	
28.8	What is a fuel cell?	
28.9	What are the products in a hydrogen fuel cell?	
28.10	State three advantages of hydrogen fuel cells	
28.11	State three disadvantages of hydrogen fuel cells	
28.12	Give the overall equation in a hydrogen fuel cell	

ANSWER KEY

29.1	What is an alkene?	A hydrocarbon with a double bond
29.2	What is the general formula for alkenes?	C_nH_{2n}
29.3	What does unsaturated means?	Contains double bonds (which could become C-H bonds)
29.4	What are the first four alkenes?	Ethene, propene, butene, pentene
29.5	What are the four reactions of alkenes?	Combustion, with water, with hydrogen and with halogens
29.6	How is the combustion of alkenes different to combustion of alkanes?	Alkenes usually react by incomplete combustion so burn with smoky flames
29.7	Why are the reactions of alkenes with hydrogen, water and halogens known as "addition" reactions?	Because new atoms are being added to the molecule by breaking the double bond
29.8	What is the product from the reaction of an alkene with hydrogen?	An alkane
29.9	What conditions are necessary in the reaction of alkenes with hydrogen?	60°C, Nickel catalyst
29.10	What is the product from the reaction of an alkene with a halogen?	An alkane with two halogen atoms where the double bond used to be
29.11	What is the product from the reaction of an alkene with steam?	An alcohol
29.12	What conditions are necessary for the reaction of alkenes with steam?	High temperature, high pressure, catalyst

TRACKER

Quiz	Date	Score
1		
2		
3		
4		
5		
6		

Got it? ☐

29.1	What is an alkene?	
29.2	What is the general formula for alkenes?	
29.3	What does unsaturated means?	
29.4	What are the first four alkenes?	
29.5	What are the four reactions of alkenes?	
29.6	How is the combustion of alkenes different to combustion of alkanes?	
29.7	Why are the reactions of alkenes with hydrogen, water and halogens known as "addition" reactions?	
29.8	What is the product from the reaction of an alkene with hydrogen?	
29.9	What conditions are necessary in the reaction of alkenes with hydrogen?	
29.10	What is the product from the reaction of an alkene with a halogen?	
29.11	What is the product from the reaction of an alkene with steam?	
29.12	What conditions are necessary for the reaction of alkenes with steam?	

Section 29: Further Organic - Alkenes (*Triple Content*)

29.1	What is an alkene?	
29.2	What is the general formula for alkenes?	
29.3	What does unsaturated means?	
29.4	What are the first four alkenes?	
29.5	What are the four reactions of alkenes?	
29.6	How is the combustion of alkenes different to combustion of alkanes?	
29.7	Why are the reactions of alkenes with hydrogen, water and halogens known as "addition" reactions?	
29.8	What is the product from the reaction of an alkene with hydrogen?	
29.9	What conditions are necessary in the reaction of alkenes with hydrogen?	
29.10	What is the product from the reaction of an alkene with a halogen?	
29.11	What is the product from the reaction of an alkene with steam?	
29.12	What conditions are necessary for the reaction of alkenes with steam?	

29.1	What is an alkene?	
29.2	What is the general formula for alkenes?	
29.3	What does unsaturated means?	
29.4	What are the first four alkenes?	
29.5	What are the four reactions of alkenes?	
29.6	How is the combustion of alkenes different to combustion of alkanes?	
29.7	Why are the reactions of alkenes with hydrogen, water and halogens known as "addition" reactions?	
29.8	What is the product from the reaction of an alkene with hydrogen?	
29.9	What conditions are necessary in the reaction of alkenes with hydrogen?	
29.10	What is the product from the reaction of an alkene with a halogen?	
29.11	What is the product from the reaction of an alkene with steam?	
29.12	What conditions are necessary for the reaction of alkenes with steam?	

Section 29: Further Organic - Alkenes (*Triple Content*)

29.1	What is an alkene?	
29.2	What is the general formula for alkenes?	
29.3	What does unsaturated means?	
29.4	What are the first four alkenes?	
29.5	What are the four reactions of alkenes?	
29.6	How is the combustion of alkenes different to combustion of alkanes?	
29.7	Why are the reactions of alkenes with hydrogen, water and halogens known as "addition" reactions?	
29.8	What is the product from the reaction of an alkene with hydrogen?	
29.9	What conditions are necessary in the reaction of alkenes with hydrogen?	
29.10	What is the product from the reaction of an alkene with a halogen?	
29.11	What is the product from the reaction of an alkene with steam?	
29.12	What conditions are necessary for the reaction of alkenes with steam?	

Section 29: Further Organic - Alkenes (*Triple Content*)

29.1	What is an alkene?	
29.2	What is the general formula for alkenes?	
29.3	What does unsaturated means?	
29.4	What are the first four alkenes?	
29.5	What are the four reactions of alkenes?	
29.6	How is the combustion of alkenes different to combustion of alkanes?	
29.7	Why are the reactions of alkenes with hydrogen, water and halogens known as "addition" reactions?	
29.8	What is the product from the reaction of an alkene with hydrogen?	
29.9	What conditions are necessary in the reaction of alkenes with hydrogen?	
29.10	What is the product from the reaction of an alkene with a halogen?	
29.11	What is the product from the reaction of an alkene with steam?	
29.12	What conditions are necessary for the reaction of alkenes with steam?	

29.1	What is an alkene?	
29.2	What is the general formula for alkenes?	
29.3	What does unsaturated means?	
29.4	What are the first four alkenes?	
29.5	What are the four reactions of alkenes?	
29.6	How is the combustion of alkenes different to combustion of alkanes?	
29.7	Why are the reactions of alkenes with hydrogen, water and halogens known as "addition" reactions?	
29.8	What is the product from the reaction of an alkene with hydrogen?	
29.9	What conditions are necessary in the reaction of alkenes with hydrogen?	
29.10	What is the product from the reaction of an alkene with a halogen?	
29.11	What is the product from the reaction of an alkene with steam?	
29.12	What conditions are necessary for the reaction of alkenes with steam?	

ANSWER KEY

30.1	What functional group do all alcohols have?	OH
30.2	Name the first four alcohols	Methanol, ethanol, propanol, butanol
30.3	What happens when an alcohol reacts with sodium?	It forms a sodium salt (e.g. sodium ethoxide from ethanol) and releases hydrogen gas.
30.4	What are the products of a combustion reaction involving an alcohol and oxygen?	Carbon dioxide and water
30.5	Do alcohols dissolve in water?	Yes, they form neutral solutions
30.6	How do alcohols react with oxidizing agents?	They turn into carboxylic acids
30.7	What are the main uses of alcohols?	Solvents, ethanol used as drinking alcohol and a biofuel
30.8	What is fermentation?	The process of turning glucose (a natural sugar) into ethanol
30.9	What is required for natural fermentation?	Yeast
30.10	What functional groups do all carboxylic acids have?	COOH
30.11	Name the first four carboxylic acids	Methanoic acid, ethanoic acid, propanoic acid, butanoic acid
30.12	What is the product of a reaction between an alcohol and a carboxylic acid?	An ester

TRACKER

Quiz	Date	Score
1		
2		
3		
4		
5		
6		

Got it? ☐

30.1	What functional group do all alcohols have?	
30.2	Name the first four alcohols	
30.3	What happens when an alcohol reacts with sodium?	
30.4	What are the products of a combustion reaction involving an alcohol and oxygen?	
30.5	Do alcohols dissolve in water?	
30.6	How do alcohols react with oxidizing agents?	
30.7	What are the main uses of alcohols?	
30.8	What is fermentation?	
30.9	What is required for natural fermentation?	
30.10	What functional groups do all carboxylic acids have?	
30.11	Name the first four carboxylic acids	
30.12	What is the product of a reaction between an alcohol and a carboxylic acid?	

30.1	What functional group do all alcohols have?	
30.2	Name the first four alcohols	
30.3	What happens when an alcohol reacts with sodium?	
30.4	What are the products of a combustion reaction involving an alcohol and oxygen?	
30.5	Do alcohols dissolve in water?	
30.6	How do alcohols react with oxidizing agents?	
30.7	What are the main uses of alcohols?	
30.8	What is fermentation?	
30.9	What is required for natural fermentation?	
30.10	What functional groups do all carboxylic acids have?	
30.11	Name the first four carboxylic acids	
30.12	What is the product of a reaction between an alcohol and a carboxylic acid?	

30.1	What functional group do all alcohols have?	
30.2	Name the first four alcohols	
30.3	What happens when an alcohol reacts with sodium?	
30.4	What are the products of a combustion reaction involving an alcohol and oxygen?	
30.5	Do alcohols dissolve in water?	
30.6	How do alcohols react with oxidizing agents?	
30.7	What are the main uses of alcohols?	
30.8	What is fermentation?	
30.9	What is required for natural fermentation?	
30.10	What functional groups do all carboxylic acids have?	
30.11	Name the first four carboxylic acids	
30.12	What is the product of a reaction between an alcohol and a carboxylic acid?	

30.1	What functional group do all alcohols have?	
30.2	Name the first four alcohols	
30.3	What happens when an alcohol reacts with sodium?	
30.4	What are the products of a combustion reaction involving an alcohol and oxygen?	
30.5	Do alcohols dissolve in water?	
30.6	How do alcohols react with oxidizing agents?	
30.7	What are the main uses of alcohols?	
30.8	What is fermentation?	
30.9	What is required for natural fermentation?	
30.10	What functional groups do all carboxylic acids have?	
30.11	Name the first four carboxylic acids	
30.12	What is the product of a reaction between an alcohol and a carboxylic acid?	

30.1	What functional group do all alcohols have?	
30.2	Name the first four alcohols	
30.3	What happens when an alcohol reacts with sodium?	
30.4	What are the products of a combustion reaction involving an alcohol and oxygen?	
30.5	Do alcohols dissolve in water?	
30.6	How do alcohols react with oxidizing agents?	
30.7	What are the main uses of alcohols?	
30.8	What is fermentation?	
30.9	What is required for natural fermentation?	
30.10	What functional groups do all carboxylic acids have?	
30.11	Name the first four carboxylic acids	
30.12	What is the product of a reaction between an alcohol and a carboxylic acid?	

30.1	What functional group do all alcohols have?	
30.2	Name the first four alcohols	
30.3	What happens when an alcohol reacts with sodium?	
30.4	What are the products of a combustion reaction involving an alcohol and oxygen?	
30.5	Do alcohols dissolve in water?	
30.6	How do alcohols react with oxidizing agents?	
30.7	What are the main uses of alcohols?	
30.8	What is fermentation?	
30.9	What is required for natural fermentation?	
30.10	What functional groups do all carboxylic acids have?	
30.11	Name the first four carboxylic acids	
30.12	What is the product of a reaction between an alcohol and a carboxylic acid?	

ANSWER KEY

31.1	What is polymerisation?	The process of using small molecules (monomers) to make long chain molecules (polymers)
31.2	What are the two types of polymerisation?	Addition and condensation
31.3	What monomers are involved in addition polymerisation?	Alkenes
31.4	What type of monomers are involved in condensation polymerisation?	Ones with two functional groups (like a diol)
31.5	What are the products of condensation polymerisation?	A polymer and a small molecule (usually water)
31.6	What is an amino acid?	A biological molecule with two functional groups
31.7	Which functional groups do amino acids have?	NH_2 and -COOH
31.8	What do amino acids form during a condensation reaction?	Polypeptides
31.9	What is formed from different amino acids combined in one chain?	Proteins
31.10	What does DNA stand for?	Deoxyribonucleic acid
31.11	Name four naturally occurring polymers	DNA, proteins, starch, cellulose
31.12	What monomers are starch and cellulose made of?	Glucose

TRACKER

Quiz	Date	Score
1		
2		
3		
4		
5		
6		

Got it? ☐

31.1	What is polymerisation?	
31.2	What are the two types of polymerisation?	
31.3	What monomers are involved in addition polymerisation?	
31.4	What type of monomers are involved in condensation polymerisation?	
31.5	What are the products of condensation polymerisation?	
31.6	What is an amino acid?	
31.7	Which functional groups do amino acids have?	
31.8	What do amino acids form during a condensation reaction?	
31.9	What is formed from different amino acids combined in one chain?	
31.10	What does DNA stand for?	
31.11	Name four naturally occurring polymers	
31.12	What monomers are starch and cellulose made of?	

31.1	What is polymerisation?	
31.2	What are the two types of polymerisation?	
31.3	What monomers are involved in addition polymerisation?	
31.4	What type of monomers are involved in condensation polymerisation?	
31.5	What are the products of condensation polymerisation?	
31.6	What is an amino acid?	
31.7	Which functional groups do amino acids have?	
31.8	What do amino acids form during a condensation reaction?	
31.9	What is formed from different amino acids combined in one chain?	
31.10	What does DNA stand for?	
31.11	Name four naturally occurring polymers	
31.12	What monomers are starch and cellulose made of?	

31.1	What is polymerisation?	
31.2	What are the two types of polymerisation?	
31.3	What monomers are involved in addition polymerisation?	
31.4	What type of monomers are involved in condensation polymerisation?	
31.5	What are the products of condensation polymerisation?	
31.6	What is an amino acid?	
31.7	Which functional groups do amino acids have?	
31.8	What do amino acids form during a condensation reaction?	
31.9	What is formed from different amino acids combined in one chain?	
31.10	What does DNA stand for?	
31.11	Name four naturally occurring polymers	
31.12	What monomers are starch and cellulose made of?	

31.1	What is polymerisation?	
31.2	What are the two types of polymerisation?	
31.3	What monomers are involved in addition polymerisation?	
31.4	What type of monomers are involved in condensation polymerisation?	
31.5	What are the products of condensation polymerisation?	
31.6	What is an amino acid?	
31.7	Which functional groups do amino acids have?	
31.8	What do amino acids form during a condensation reaction?	
31.9	What is formed from different amino acids combined in one chain?	
31.10	What does DNA stand for?	
31.11	Name four naturally occurring polymers	
31.12	What monomers are starch and cellulose made of?	

31.1	What is polymerisation?	
31.2	What are the two types of polymerisation?	
31.3	What monomers are involved in addition polymerisation?	
31.4	What type of monomers are involved in condensation polymerisation?	
31.5	What are the products of condensation polymerisation?	
31.6	What is an amino acid?	
31.7	Which functional groups do amino acids have?	
31.8	What do amino acids form during a condensation reaction?	
31.9	What is formed from different amino acids combined in one chain?	
31.10	What does DNA stand for?	
31.11	Name four naturally occurring polymers	
31.12	What monomers are starch and cellulose made of?	

31.1	What is polymerisation?	
31.2	What are the two types of polymerisation?	
31.3	What monomers are involved in addition polymerisation?	
31.4	What type of monomers are involved in condensation polymerisation?	
31.5	What are the products of condensation polymerisation?	
31.6	What is an amino acid?	
31.7	Which functional groups do amino acids have?	
31.8	What do amino acids form during a condensation reaction?	
31.9	What is formed from different amino acids combined in one chain?	
31.10	What does DNA stand for?	
31.11	Name four naturally occurring polymers	
31.12	What monomers are starch and cellulose made of?	

Section 32: Identification of Ions 1 (*Triple Content*)

ANSWER KEY

32.1	What is a flame test?	A test to identify metal ions (cations)
32.2	What is the colour of the flame produced from compounds containing: lithium, sodium, potassium, calcium, copper	Crimson, yellow, lilac, orange-red, green
32.3	Which solutions produce white precipitates on addition of sodium hydroxide?	Solutions containing aluminium, magnesium, calcium ions
32.4	How can a solution of aluminium ions be distinguished from calcium and magnesium ones?	Its precipitate will dissolve in excess sodium hydroxide
32.5	What is the colour of the precipitate formed from the addition of sodium hydroxide to a solution containing copper (II) ions?	Blue
32.6	What is the colour of the precipitate formed from the addition of sodium hydroxide to a solution containing iron(II) ions?	Green
32.7	What is the colour of the precipitate formed from the addition of sodium hydroxide to a solution containing iron(III) ions?	Brown
32.8	What is the test for carbonates?	Add an acid to generate carbon dioxide gas
32.9	What is the test for halides?	Add silver nitrate and nitric acid to generate a solid silver halide precipitate
32.10	What are the colours of the silver halides?	Silver chloride white, silver bromide cream, silver iodide yellow
32.11	What is the test for sulfate ions?	Add barium chloride and hydrochloric acid, forms white precipitate
32.12	What is an instrumental method?	Use of scientific technology to perform chemical analysis

TRACKER

Quiz	Date	Score
1		
2		
3		
4		
5		
6		

Got it? ☐

32.1	What is a flame test?	
32.2	What is the colour of the flame produced from compounds containing: lithium, sodium, potassium, calcium, copper	
32.3	Which solutions produce white precipitates on addition of sodium hydroxide?	
32.4	How can a solution of aluminium ions be distinguished from calcium and magnesium ones?	
32.5	What is the colour of the precipitate formed from the addition of sodium hydroxide to a solution containing copper (II) ions?	
32.6	What is the colour of the precipitate formed from the addition of sodium hydroxide to a solution containing iron(II) ions?	
32.7	What is the colour of the precipitate formed from the addition of sodium hydroxide to a solution containing iron(III) ions?	
32.8	What is the test for carbonates?	
32.9	What is the test for halides?	
32.10	What are the colours of the silver halides?	
32.11	What is the test for sulfate ions?	
32.12	What is an instrumental method?	

Section 32: Identification of Ions 1 (*Triple Content*)

32.1	What is a flame test?	
32.2	What is the colour of the flame produced from compounds containing: lithium, sodium, potassium, calcium, copper	
32.3	Which solutions produce white precipitates on addition of sodium hydroxide?	
32.4	How can a solution of aluminium ions be distinguished from calcium and magnesium ones?	
32.5	What is the colour of the precipitate formed from the addition of sodium hydroxide to a solution containing copper (II) ions?	
32.6	What is the colour of the precipitate formed from the addition of sodium hydroxide to a solution containing iron(II) ions?	
32.7	What is the colour of the precipitate formed from the addition of sodium hydroxide to a solution containing iron(III) ions?	
32.8	What is the test for carbonates?	
32.9	What is the test for halides?	
32.10	What are the colours of the silver halides?	
32.11	What is the test for sulfate ions?	
32.12	What is an instrumental method?	

32.1	What is a flame test?	
32.2	What is the colour of the flame produced from compounds containing: lithium, sodium, potassium, calcium, copper	
32.3	Which solutions produce white precipitates on addition of sodium hydroxide?	
32.4	How can a solution of aluminium ions be distinguished from calcium and magnesium ones?	
32.5	What is the colour of the precipitate formed from the addition of sodium hydroxide to a solution containing copper (II) ions?	
32.6	What is the colour of the precipitate formed from the addition of sodium hydroxide to a solution containing iron(II) ions?	
32.7	What is the colour of the precipitate formed from the addition of sodium hydroxide to a solution containing iron(III) ions?	
32.8	What is the test for carbonates?	
32.9	What is the test for halides?	
32.10	What are the colours of the silver halides?	
32.11	What is the test for sulfate ions?	
32.12	What is an instrumental method?	

32.1	What is a flame test?	
32.2	What is the colour of the flame produced from compounds containing: lithium, sodium, potassium, calcium, copper	
32.3	Which solutions produce white precipitates on addition of sodium hydroxide?	
32.4	How can a solution of aluminium ions be distinguished from calcium and magnesium ones?	
32.5	What is the colour of the precipitate formed from the addition of sodium hydroxide to a solution containing copper (II) ions?	
32.6	What is the colour of the precipitate formed from the addition of sodium hydroxide to a solution containing iron(II) ions?	
32.7	What is the colour of the precipitate formed from the addition of sodium hydroxide to a solution containing iron(III) ions?	
32.8	What is the test for carbonates?	
32.9	What is the test for halides?	
32.10	What are the colours of the silver halides?	
32.11	What is the test for sulfate ions?	
32.12	What is an instrumental method?	

32.1	What is a flame test?	
32.2	What is the colour of the flame produced from compounds containing: lithium, sodium, potassium, calcium, copper	
32.3	Which solutions produce white precipitates on addition of sodium hydroxide?	
32.4	How can a solution of aluminium ions be distinguished from calcium and magnesium ones?	
32.5	What is the colour of the precipitate formed from the addition of sodium hydroxide to a solution containing copper (II) ions?	
32.6	What is the colour of the precipitate formed from the addition of sodium hydroxide to a solution containing iron(II) ions?	
32.7	What is the colour of the precipitate formed from the addition of sodium hydroxide to a solution containing iron(III) ions?	
32.8	What is the test for carbonates?	
32.9	What is the test for halides?	
32.10	What are the colours of the silver halides?	
32.11	What is the test for sulfate ions?	
32.12	What is an instrumental method?	

32.1	What is a flame test?	
32.2	What is the colour of the flame produced from compounds containing: lithium, sodium, potassium, calcium, copper	
32.3	Which solutions produce white precipitates on addition of sodium hydroxide?	
32.4	How can a solution of aluminium ions be distinguished from calcium and magnesium ones?	
32.5	What is the colour of the precipitate formed from the addition of sodium hydroxide to a solution containing copper (II) ions?	
32.6	What is the colour of the precipitate formed from the addition of sodium hydroxide to a solution containing iron(II) ions?	
32.7	What is the colour of the precipitate formed from the addition of sodium hydroxide to a solution containing iron(III) ions?	
32.8	What is the test for carbonates?	
32.9	What is the test for halides?	
32.10	What are the colours of the silver halides?	
32.11	What is the test for sulfate ions?	
32.12	What is an instrumental method?	

ANSWER KEY

33.1	What are the three advantages of instrumental methods?	They are accurate (gives correct results), sensitive (only needs a small sample to work), rapid (a lot faster than other tests)
33.2	What is flame emission spectroscopy?	An instrumental analysis tool for identifying metal ions
33.3	How is flame emissions spectroscopy carried out?	Sample placed in a flame, light emitted is passed through a spectroscope to give a spectrum which can be compared to a reference
33.4	What is corrosion?	The destruction of materials by chemical reactions with substances in the environment
33.5	What is necessary for rusting to occur?	Presence of air and water
33.6	How can corrosion be prevented?	By use of a barrier coating or sacrificial protection coating
33.7	Give three examples of barrier coatings	Greasing, painting, electroplating
33.8	How does sacrifical protection work?	A more reactive metal is corroded rather than the base metal
33.9	Name two types of glass	Soda-lime glass and borosilicate glass
33.10	How are clay ceramics made?	Shaping wet clay and heating in a furnace
33.11	What do the properties of polymers depend on?	The monomers they are made of and the conditions under which they are made
33.12	What is the difference between thermosetting and thermosoftening polymers?	Thermosoftening ones melt when they are heated, thermosetting do not

TRACKER

Quiz	Date	Score
1		
2		
3		
4		
5		
6		

Got it? ☐

33.1	What are the three advantages of instrumental methods?	
33.2	What is flame emission spectroscopy?	
33.3	How is flame emissions spectroscopy carried out?	
33.4	What is corrosion?	
33.5	What is necessary for rusting to occur?	
33.6	How can corrosion be prevented?	
33.7	Give three examples of barrier coatings	
33.8	How does sacrifical protection work?	
33.9	Name two types of glass	
33.10	How are clay ceramics made?	
33.11	What do the properties of polymers depend on?	
33.12	What is the difference between thermosetting and thermosoftening polymers?	

33.1	What are the three advantages of instrumental methods?	
33.2	What is flame emission spectroscopy?	
33.3	How is flame emissions spectroscopy carried out?	
33.4	What is corrosion?	
33.5	What is necessary for rusting to occur?	
33.6	How can corrosion be prevented?	
33.7	Give three examples of barrier coatings	
33.8	How does sacrifical protection work?	
33.9	Name two types of glass	
33.10	How are clay ceramics made?	
33.11	What do the properties of polymers depend on?	
33.12	What is the difference between thermosetting and thermosoftening polymers?	

33.1	What are the three advantages of instrumental methods?	
33.2	What is flame emission spectroscopy?	
33.3	How is flame emissions spectroscopy carried out?	
33.4	What is corrosion?	
33.5	What is necessary for rusting to occur?	
33.6	How can corrosion be prevented?	
33.7	Give three examples of barrier coatings	
33.8	How does sacrifical protection work?	
33.9	Name two types of glass	
33.10	How are clay ceramics made?	
33.11	What do the properties of polymers depend on?	
33.12	What is the difference between thermosetting and thermosoftening polymers?	

33.1	What are the three advantages of instrumental methods?	
33.2	What is flame emission spectroscopy?	
33.3	How is flame emissions spectroscopy carried out?	
33.4	What is corrosion?	
33.5	What is necessary for rusting to occur?	
33.6	How can corrosion be prevented?	
33.7	Give three examples of barrier coatings	
33.8	How does sacrifical protection work?	
33.9	Name two types of glass	
33.10	How are clay ceramics made?	
33.11	What do the properties of polymers depend on?	
33.12	What is the difference between thermosetting and thermosoftening polymers?	

33.1	What are the three advantages of instrumental methods?	
33.2	What is flame emission spectroscopy?	
33.3	How is flame emissions spectroscopy carried out?	
33.4	What is corrosion?	
33.5	What is necessary for rusting to occur?	
33.6	How can corrosion be prevented?	
33.7	Give three examples of barrier coatings	
33.8	How does sacrifical protection work?	
33.9	Name two types of glass	
33.10	How are clay ceramics made?	
33.11	What do the properties of polymers depend on?	
33.12	What is the difference between thermosetting and thermosoftening polymers?	

33.1	What are the three advantages of instrumental methods?	
33.2	What is flame emission spectroscopy?	
33.3	How is flame emissions spectroscopy carried out?	
33.4	What is corrosion?	
33.5	What is necessary for rusting to occur?	
33.6	How can corrosion be prevented?	
33.7	Give three examples of barrier coatings	
33.8	How does sacrifical protection work?	
33.9	Name two types of glass	
33.10	How are clay ceramics made?	
33.11	What do the properties of polymers depend on?	
33.12	What is the difference between thermosetting and thermosoftening polymers?	

Section 34: Using Materials 2 (*Triple Content*)

ANSWER KEY

34.1	Why do thermosetting polymers not melt when heated?	They have strong cross-links between the polymer chains
34.2	What is a composite?	A material made of two materials
34.3	Generally, what are the two types of materials in composites?	A matrix and a reinforcement (normally fibres or fragments)
34.4	Give an example of a composite	Reinforced concrete, plywood
34.5	What is the Haber process?	A reaction to generate ammonia from hydrogen and nitrogen
34.6	Where do the reactants for the Haber process come from?	Nitrogen: the air, Hydrogen: natural gas
34.7	What conditions are required for the Haber process?	High temperature, high pressure, iron catalyst
34.8	What is an NPK fertiliser?	A fertiliser with nitrogen, phosphorous and potassium compounds in
34.9	How must phosphate rock be treated before it can be used as a fertiliser?	Reacted with acid
34.10	What is the product of a reaction between phosphate rock and nitric, phosphoric or sulphuric acid?	Nitric acid: calcium nitrate, phosphoric acid: calcium phosphate, sulphuric acid: calcium sulphate

TRACKER

Quiz	Date	Score
1		
2		
3		
4		
5		
6		

Got it? ☐

34.1	Why do thermosetting polymers not melt when heated?	
34.2	What is a composite?	
34.3	Generally, what are the two types of materials in composites?	
34.4	Give an example of a composite	
34.5	What is the Haber process?	
34.6	Where do the reactants for the Haber process come from?	
34.7	What conditions are required for the Haber process?	
34.8	What is an NPK fertiliser?	
34.9	How must phosphate rock be treated before it can be used as a fertiliser?	
34.10	What is the product of a reaction between phosphate rock and nitric, phosphoric or sulphuric acid?	

34.1	Why do thermosetting polymers not melt when heated?	
34.2	What is a composite?	
34.3	Generally, what are the two types of materials in composites?	
34.4	Give an example of a composite	
34.5	What is the Haber process?	
34.6	Where do the reactants for the Haber process come from?	
34.7	What conditions are required for the Haber process?	
34.8	What is an NPK fertiliser?	
34.9	How must phosphate rock be treated before it can be used as a fertiliser?	
34.10	What is the product of a reaction between phosphate rock and nitric, phosphoric or sulphuric acid?	

34.1	Why do thermosetting polymers not melt when heated?	
34.2	What is a composite?	
34.3	Generally, what are the two types of materials in composites?	
34.4	Give an example of a composite	
34.5	What is the Haber process?	
34.6	Where do the reactants for the Haber process come from?	
34.7	What conditions are required for the Haber process?	
34.8	What is an NPK fertiliser?	
34.9	How must phosphate rock be treated before it can be used as a fertiliser?	
34.10	What is the product of a reaction between phosphate rock and nitric, phosphoric or sulphuric acid?	

34.1	Why do thermosetting polymers not melt when heated?	
34.2	What is a composite?	
34.3	Generally, what are the two types of materials in composites?	
34.4	Give an example of a composite	
34.5	What is the Haber process?	
34.6	Where do the reactants for the Haber process come from?	
34.7	What conditions are required for the Haber process?	
34.8	What is an NPK fertiliser?	
34.9	How must phosphate rock be treated before it can be used as a fertiliser?	
34.10	What is the product of a reaction between phosphate rock and nitric, phosphoric or sulphuric acid?	

Section 34: Using Materials 2 (*Triple Content*)

34.1	Why do thermosetting polymers not melt when heated?	
34.2	What is a composite?	
34.3	Generally, what are the two types of materials in composites?	
34.4	Give an example of a composite	
34.5	What is the Haber process?	
34.6	Where do the reactants for the Haber process come from?	
34.7	What conditions are required for the Haber process?	
34.8	What is an NPK fertiliser?	
34.9	How must phosphate rock be treated before it can be used as a fertiliser?	
34.10	What is the product of a reaction between phosphate rock and nitric, phosphoric or sulphuric acid?	

34.1	Why do thermosetting polymers not melt when heated?	
34.2	What is a composite?	
34.3	Generally, what are the two types of materials in composites?	
34.4	Give an example of a composite	
34.5	What is the Haber process?	
34.6	Where do the reactants for the Haber process come from?	
34.7	What conditions are required for the Haber process?	
34.8	What is an NPK fertiliser?	
34.9	How must phosphate rock be treated before it can be used as a fertiliser?	
34.10	What is the product of a reaction between phosphate rock and nitric, phosphoric or sulphuric acid?	